RENAISSANCE SOCIETY OF AMERICA REPRINT TEXTS 9

ON ASSISTANCE
TO THE POOR

Juan Luis Vives

Translated with an Introduction and Commentary by
Alice Tobriner, SNJM

Published by University of Toronto Press
Toronto Buffalo London
in association with the Renaissance Society of America

© Renaissance Society of America 1999
Printed in the U.S.A.
ISBN 0-8020-8289-0

Reprinted 2012

This edition is reprinted from the 1971 School of Social Service Administration, University of Chicago edition, entitled "A Sixteenth Century Urban Report. Part I Introduction and Commentary. Part II Translation of On Assistance to the Poor by Juan Luis Vives," by arrangement with The School of Social Service Administration, University of Chicago.

Printed on acid-free paper

Canadian Cataloguing in Publication Data

Vives, Juan Luis, 1492–1540
On assistance to the poor

(Renaissance Society of America reprint texts ; 9)
ISBN 0-8020-8289-0
1. Poor – Services for – Belgium – Bruges – History. 2. Bruges (Belgium) – Social conditions – 16th century. 3. Public welfare. 4. Poverty.   I. Tobriner, Alice, 1922–   .   II. Renaissance Society of America.   III. Title.   IV. Series.

HT115.V58 1999   301.363   C99-930367-8

EDITOR'S PREFACE

"I wish we were able to eliminate poverty completely in this city." How many community leaders and public officials have let that thought enter their minds, at least fleetingly, only to cast it out again as unrealistic, impossible, or almost unthinkable! Yet Juan Luis Vives, the transplanted Spanish humanist, dared include such a statement in his communication addressed to the Town Council and Senate of Bruges in 1526. To his writing Vives brought the observations made during fourteen years' residence in Bruges and the perspective gained through an unusual education in Valencia. He also brought profound human understanding, as evidenced in his comments on the mentally ill.

Sister Alice Tobriner, who wrote the "Introduction and Commentary" and prepared the new translation of *De Subventione Pauperum,*[1] first became acquainted with Vives during her doctoral study at Stanford University. Her thesis, entitled "J. L. Vives' *Introduction to Wisdom,*" was published in 1968.

The student who has not encountered Vives before should find the translation of great interest. The urban problems of sixteenth-century Bruges may have been different in scale from those of today, but their content seems strangely familiar. Readers who have studied Vives will be intrigued by the introductory essay. Through careful research Sister Alice has put together the story of the link between the work of Vives and that of Sir Thomas More and other English leaders who worked on the early statutes finally incorporated into the 1601 Poor Law. How one wishes there were a recording of the conversations of Vives and Sir Thomas More as they beat out their ideas about the responsibility of government for the care of the poor!

The issues that Vives dealt with are being debated with vehemence in the twentieth century in the United States and elsewhere. It is the hope of the editors of the *Social Service Review* that a rereading of the work of Vives and of Sister Alice's thought-provoking essay may lend perspective for that debate.

Rachel Marks, Editor
SOCIAL SERVICE REVIEW

---

1. A translation of part of *De Subventione Pauperum,* by Margaret M. Sherwood, was published as "Concerning the Relief of the Poor," *Studies in Social Work,* No. 11 (New York: New York School of Philanthropy, 1917).

TABLE OF CONTENTS

PART I

INTRODUCTION AND COMMENTARY

by

Sister Alice Tobriner

A POSITION PAPER ON POVERTY, 1526

For mental recreation the modern armchair philosopher might spin out resemblances between the years of the Reformation-Renaissance Era (roughly the first half of the sixteenth century) and the first seven decades of the twentieth century. Both epochs have witnessed an enlargement of their life space through exploration, whether of the New World or of the universe; both have experienced a communications explosion, whether by the printing press or through electronic media; both have undergone a population upsurge whose numbers drifted into urban centers ill-prepared to receive the new immigrants; both felt the impact of educational theorists, larger student bodies, new academic structures, and the demand for education as a means of upward social mobility. The two ages suffered through long wars followed by scattered, debilitating brush-fire actions; both sensed the ambivalence of a hunger for religion and a rejection of churches; both stood aghast at the unforgivable conditions in which the masses attempted to live out their lives in hunger and squalor. Ironically, both were also identified as times of greatest concern for the humanism of existence.[1]

Can the subsequent history of the one predict the future of the other?

Men like Juan Luis Vives (1492-1540), staunch and vocal Roman Catholics that they were, nevertheless were fascinated by magic and the means for reading the future.[2] In his commentaries on *The City of God* (1522), for instance, Vives insisted that such practices were very wrong indeed, and then proceeded to discuss them in such detail that one suspects an actually inverted acceptance of them.[3] Much more the realist in his extensive work on education, he recommended instead the study of history as a means of presaging the future.[4] And so, taking the hint of a wise master, the twentieth-century urbanite might well look to the past life of his city and of his own people in order to discover who he is, how and why he came to his present paradox, and where he is likely to be going because of his past.

Historically, the American colonial experience developed as an English declaration of war on poverty.[5] The first three American centuries of dealing with the disadvantaged were properly paternalistic and personally distant. Now a lately-come popular concern, "poverty" has reached the college and university research level, status symbol for a questionable cause, and presently—because so many professors hold rank in the governmental agencies that issue national policy—it has entered the competition for presidential and congressional support. Pragmatists and hungry people alike proffer plans for alleviating distress, unemployment, and indigence; few search out the origins of laws that they propose to change. Aside from the moral issue of persons reduced to

3

penury, the inefficiency of never questioning the past confirms the ancient judgment: those who will not study the past will be condemned to live with its mistakes.

Juan Luis Vives of Bruges published *On Assistance to the Poor* in 1526, and for his efforts he was given a silver cup by the City Council. Probably filled with coins, such a gratuitous award was typically conferred on writers and poets who had expended some effort for wealthy patrons.[6] While some of the ideas of Vives were uniquely his own, the genius of the work lay in its distinctive development of a single integrated system out of the several practices already functioning in northern Europe. Within a short time these principles and procedures were transferred into the English poor laws and then to American colonies and states. So it follows that a man so perceptive of urban problems three centuries ago, whose works influenced the laws that need restructuring now, needs to be introduced to contemporary society.

THE TIMES AND THE PROPOSALS

The early 1500s sensed an urgency in accumulating urban problems: migration, overpopulation, crime, and inadequate education. While the latter-day delineation of these concerns may differ from that of this very era, for purposes of the good life within a well-ordered community the problems were as threatening and deep-seated then as in the twentieth century. In the very years in which Vives was thinking and writing about relief to the poor, the noblemen and peasants of Germany were locked in a bitter struggle for land and religion. In England Wolsey had already introduced a more binding "enclosure system" than before, in spite of the protests lodged ten years before in Thomas More's *Utopia*. The French monarchy was demanding exorbitant taxes in order to support its anti-Hapsburg wars, as well as to ransom the clumsy sons of Francis I, who had allowed themselves to be captured by Imperial forces. Throughout western Europe the harvests in the mid-1520s had been meager, and prices had been inflated until there was economic chaos. Religious turmoil bubbled like a witches' brew threatening to poison the entire body of Christiandom, as indeed it did eventually. Charles V had sent his troops into Rome, not commanding but not forbidding the destruction wreaked by unrestrained mercenaries, while Clement VII was huddling in his prison, humiliated, chagrined, exposed finally and irrevocably as an ineffective leader in either the Reformation or renewal of the spirit of the Church.[7]

A new urban society provided the matrix of change from a medieval to an early modern government.[8] In England political theory shifted the source of authority from God to the King.[9] For the individual, increasing confidence in the power of the human will was substituted for the older, unquestioning confidence in divine, papal, and royal prerogatives. The concept of the state as an independent body politic possessing newly defined rights and responsibilities existed only in seminal form when Vives penned the first chapter heading of Book 2, "The Obligations of the Administrator of the City toward the Poor."

In addition to his role as political generalist, Vives wrote as an urban particularist as well.[10] For example, he noted the specifics of poverty and its effects with distinctly modern insight. A government has numerous reasons for working against poverty, he suggested, but the very survival of the state is questionable if it neglects this issue. The weak of the commonwealth cannot be ignored without a debilitating effect upon the strong. Men without means fill with resentment when they are confronted with the inequity of their position vis-à-vis the affluence of the wealthy. Inevitably, poverty incites riots, civil wars, and widespread hate between the Haves and the Have-nots. For its own benefit the state ought not to allow a condition of widespread unemployment to develop; to the contrary, universal employment acts as security against inroads into national strength and unity. Indeed, the Spanish humanist asserted that the responsibility for social disorder and individual crimes can even be imputed to the state if it remains steadfast in refusing to deal with a consistent condition of unemployment. The state should be far more concerned about the conditions that eventuate in good citizenship and internal peace than in the short-term issue of the punishment and restraint of evil-doers.

Vives recognized that some attempts had already been made in the direction of the larger solutions: taxes had been eased, public lands had been made available to the poor for raising basic foodstuffs, and certain surplus funds had been distributed to the destitute. However, he insisted, a fully organized system of relief would be required rather than individual and isolated acts of government out of context from an overall program.

To solve the problem, its elements must be identified; hence, a census of the poor must be taken. While some objection might be made about the invasion of government into the privacy of individual citizens (Vives would have had the census-takers survey the poor in their own physical milieu), it must be recognized that there is nothing so independent of the state that it is not subject to inquiry by those in the government. Both property and life are subject to the supervision and regulation of the state, insofar as both are received by, and maintained through, the cooperation of the state.

With statistics and factual surveys available, Vives advanced to coordinating poor-relief into a well-regulated, multipronged effort:

1. The poor must not remain unemployed. If they cannot find work by themselves, then the state must work with private industry in order to place them at jobs. Or, more effectively, contracts can be let to private business for the manufacture of products necessary for operating the state; in turn, such employers will use the poor as laborers. Public works provide employment opportunities—such as the construction of sewers, ditches, and buildings—to the mutual benefit of the government and the individual indigent.

2. Ordinarily, immigrants should not be allowed to enter the state because of the competition for opportunities for employment. However, exception should be made in favor of refugees from war and from areas in which the devastation

of conflict gives no hope of support for the poor.

3. Support from private sources must be invited and encouraged in order to supplement the work of the state.

4. Centers for assistance to the poor should be constructed, not for administration, but for physical support, such as a home in which individuals can be temporarily housed and assisted until they have settled into their jobs.

5. Widespread blindness in the sixteenth century enlarged the basic problem of indigence. Ordinarily cast aside as nonproductive flotsam in the stream of urban refuse, the blind with talent for specialized work must be employed as a hidden asset insufficiently developed. Some might even be sent to study, if they showed aptness.

6. The unemployed elderly and infirm would also become productive members of society if jobs suited to their condition were made available. Sheer idleness would profit neither them nor the nation.

7. Vives's prescriptions for the mentally ill were too advanced for his times. Although he addressed himself to the problem as a socioeconomic evil (the psychotic would undoubtedly have filled some ranks of the poor), his advice followed medical and psychological directions. Six years hence, he was to write one of his most famous treatises, *On the Mind,* which was seminally influential in its proffered solutions to a perennial human situation.

In the first place, the psychosis should be diagnosed in order to make a prognosis for recovery. Second, the patient should be given proper treatment. No hint of mocking, excitement, or instigation should be allowed; some unbalanced minds might actually be driven over the brink into insanity by treatment that flaunted a man's flaws in his face.

Remedies appropriate for the individual case should be applied: for some, therapy would combine appropriate work with physical nourishment; others would need mild and friendly handling so that, like wild animals, they might be gentled; others would need direct instruction about their condition; some would require forcible restraint, but it should be applied only so that they would not become the more violent. Above all, tranquillity must be introduced into their minds because it would be through serenity that reason and sanity would return. Intuitively, Vives foresaw modern medicine's boon to psychotic and neurotic alike in the chemical tranquilizers that would induce the quietude necessary for reorienting the person toward reality.

Only the twentieth century brought to fruition these radical concepts, and even then with reluctance.

8. The poor in their homes should also receive sufficient assistance to keep them from taking to the streets for support.

9. Whenever a man's income from employment will not provide sufficiently for his basic needs, the state ought to provide the money needed.

10. The attitude of those working directly with the poor should be one of understanding and acceptance. The only excuse for official intimidation of the poor, according to this mild sixteenth-century law-and-order man, lay in the refractory and unmanageable criticism of the government.

On the other hand, it is crucial that no persons external to the civic administration be allowed to influence the distribution of assistance to the poor. If the administrators were to observe such interference, their strictest penalties should be imposed upon the violators. Overseers might make recommendations in a given case upon private information received; however, their own investigations, rather than intrusions from the private source, should dominate official decisions.

Succeeding chapters enlarge the scope of poor-relief. In a short but succinct development on assistance for the children of the poor, Vives's first move would be to provide a hospital or orphanage for those abandoned. If the mother were known, the children would be reared by her until their sixth year. At that time they would be remanded to a school that would teach them letters and morals. In this permanent residence they would live in an atmosphere of frugality and cleanliness with the objective of transferring and cultivating a similar mode of thinking and acting.

Vives departed radically from accepted norms in his proposal for the education of girls, even to the point of suggesting advanced studies for those who seemed intellectually talented. His design for the teacher of inner-city children in the sixteenth century was totally distinctive: administrators were to spare no expense to secure the best of teachers in order to provide a superior education for these children, "for there can be nothing of greater danger for the sons of the poor than a cheap, inferior, and demoralizing education."

In their political organizations, ancient Greeks and Romans had the censor, an office with unique origins in tribal life. In a simplistic imitation of these ideal nations, Vives suggested censors for Bruges, not only of the poor, but of the wealthy, in order to secure the highest ethical standards for all members of the state. Watchdog committees and independent consumer crusaders suggest an analogy for contemporary times.

The financing of assistance to the poor posed as much a problem for Vives as for urban America. He referred disparagingly to the conduct of bishops and commented almost bitterly on the conditions in ecclesiastical circles which called for reform. He suggested that wealthy institutions assist the poorer ones, even in distant places.

Only "overseers" of the most integral character were to be appointed to monitor the actual distribution of money, whether it was willed, donated, or gathered from the "little boxes" placed in several of the churches. In the latter case, efforts should be made to collect only what would be necessary, rather than to accumulate large stores of money that would lead to the very problems Vives saw before him as he wrote. Almsgiving must always be voluntary; its very definition demanded this element. In view of the development of the English laws, wherein the individual parishioner was placed under the strongest psychological pressures if he did not make contributions, one notes Vives's insistence on individual freedom when giving to the less fortunate.

Finally, because the Spanish humanist found in the supernatural the roots for all his concern and respect for the tangible world, he suggested that the poor adopt an attitude of loving dependence on their Heavenly Father, who would not care for the birds of the air any less than for His children. Nor were these poor to build up provisions of wealth since Providence was even then making ready their relief. While this pious attitude seems removed from the reality of the American scene, note must be made of its reference to "those who are not in actual distress," as opposed to those suffering the immediate exigencies of poverty.

Still another category of poor was to be recognized, the poor who had come suddenly to penury (as opposed to living in it as a way of life). These, too, would require assistance—those held prisoners of war; imprisoned for debt; shipwrecked; deprived of goods through fire, floods, or disease; stripped of body and self through prostitution—in a word, all who had unexpectedly come to poverty. In many cases such deprivation would be hidden; hence, the state should provide some subtle means for discovering these needs. Subsequently, the administration of assistance must be performed in such a manner that the individual's pride would not be so wounded as to cause him to regret his acceptance of the help needed. His misery would suffice without the added barb of condescension.

Vives resignedly understood that not all of his suggested reforms would be implemented. He suspected that a typical cause underlying their rejection centered in a resistance to innovation as such; in such a case, he ingenuously suggested offering a moderate proposal at the beginning of the program. He remained convinced that eventually and gradually the more radical measures closer to his intent might be introduced, once the fear of the new had been overcome. Those who predictably would object to these concepts included the ecclesiastics—hypocrites who preached poverty and practiced the contrary; those in public office who approved of nothing except what they had themselves proposed; the poor themselves; and those ousted from office by the proposals outlined.

In the mode of traditional Christian charity, measures like these would undoubtedly win the blessing of God for individuals. Even more significant to the present essay, Vives pointed to specific benefits that flow directly to the state from such assistance to the poor. Fewer crimes would be committed; peace and social tranquility would evolve; the very physical condition of the city would be healthier and safer; laws would be respected; riots and revolutions would diminish; the education of the young would lead to future self-supporting citizens; men would be able to live in conditions rightfully a man's because of his nature; other states would imitate what Bruges had done; private individuals or other states would send their alms to be distributed through Bruges, since they could see the care with which funds were channeled to those who needed assistance.

Working papers submitted to governmental authorities, like Vives's *On Assistance to the Poor,* often find their greatest significance in the trends that develop in the lower echelons of authority because of positions adapted from the work. Actually, Bruges did not adopt any of the Vives proposals until

1556—years in which political and social machinations wreaked havoc on a city attempting to play the role of enlightened social innovator—and Vives's work was far more influential in the England of Henry and Elizabeth and in the American nation yet to develop across the seas.

WORKS IN A SIMILAR VEIN

When he penned his *On Assistance to the Poor*, Juan Luis Vives did not remain a solitary social philosopher.[11] The Council of the city of Ypres promulgated its principles in December of 1525, although apparently the statutes were already in effect as early as September of that year. In Germany, Luther summarized the work that cities had been slowly organizing in their assistance to the poor. Altenburg, Nuremburg, Strassburg, Regensburg, Kitzinger, Magdeburg, and Baden-Baden had all attempted to outlaw begging as a means of self-support among the indigent. Augsburg had its little town-within-a-town, the Fuggerei, which consisted of six streets with hospitable-looking houses offering a place of refuge for the less advantaged.

In 1523 Luther visited the town of Leisneck, where he consulted with the city fathers on a project that included ecclesiastical reforms and urban renewal. Luther described a method of administering money through the supervision of town "overseers," who would regulate the income and expenses of the "common chest." Under an innovative measure superseding the traditional alms contributed through motives of charity and unselfishness, parishioners were to be levied an obligatory tax for the welfare of the poor.

This latter measure is not, however, to be found in the ordinances issued by Zurich in 1525, "Articles Touching Almsgiving." Apparently written by Zwingli himself, the regulations called for the administration of relief to the indigent through the hands of laymen, although the cooperation of pastors was invited and desired. Begging was forbidden; voluntary donations would supplement the city's income which, at that time, was derived from the sales of suppressed monasteries and nunneries. Like Luther, Zwingli argued for a serious investigation of the needs of the poor before relief was to be authorized for them.

English efforts in these concerns came to a focus in the statutes of Parliament, as, for example, in 1531 and 1536, two series of laws undoubtedly influenced by Vives's work of 1526. Aside from the professional legislators, few laymen defended poor relief with pen and paper until after Elizabeth's first statutes had reassured the populace that assistance would continue in the same direction as that generally proposed by her father.

In the meantime, the condition of English highways had seriously deteriorated, as evidenced by the multiplication of thieves and vagabonds constantly en route to their legal places of residence. Laments and complaints began to fill the printed pages as the men of England bemoaned the conditions of indigence producing such threats to society. In 1560 John Awdeley penned the *Fraternitye of Vacabondes*,[12] while Thomas Harman probably issued his *Caveat for*

Common Cursetors vulgarly called Vacabondes, in 1566 or 1567. So popular was the latter treatise that in 1597, probably after Harman's death, some anonymous plagiarizer appropriated most of the earlier work, appended a few notes, and palmed off the popular work, *The Groundworke of Connycatching,* in 1592. The unique element about Harman's work is that he included a listing of names of "rogues and pallyards," as well as an abbreviated dictionary of terms and phrases used by the men and women of the highways, a separate vocabulary in itself.

Much more serious in composition was the *Provision for the Poore, now in Penurie, pit of the Storehouse of God's Plentie,* printed in London in 1597 by "H.A." (Henry Arthington).[13] A character-revealing sidelight on "H.A." touches on his membership in a small radical group of early-day rebels against the government. In a state that pretty well demanded almost complete obeisance to the larger policies of the government, he risked—and almost lost—his life for his revolutionary commitments. Eventually he apologized for supporting a man put to death as a traitor, and then reverted to a reactionary position from which he offered this pious, but ineffective, essay on the poor.

In 1583 such loud complaints as Philip Stubbs's *The Anatomie of Abuses* noted that the fairly large number of houses of charity caring for the ill and the poor were seriously unable to cope with the total number of such refugees from society. Another pamphlet of the day typifies a spate of documents pouring off the ordinary presses, *A Politic Plot for the Honour of the Prince, the Great Profit of the Public State, the Relief of the Poor, Preservation of the Rich, Reformation of Rogues and Idle Persons, and the Wealth of Thousands Who Know Not How to Live.*[14] The needs of the English poor were liberally represented by a vocal segment, rarely themselves members of the disadvantaged.

THE OLD PATTERNS

While some locales differed in specifics, in general the administration of assistance to the poor of Europe was not centrally organized and was not equitable.[15] Throughout most of the late medieval years, men considered it a privilege to give to the poor, if they themselves had sufficient goods of the earth. A theory of faith prevailed, based on the words of the Gospel, that if a man gave to the poor he was giving to Christ himself. In action, however, a more mechanistic attitude had entered into the once-altruistic gift-giving: if one gave to the poor, one's sins could be forgiven. In his Book 1, as well as some passages in Book 2 of his *On Assistance,* Vives reflected these sentiments, although without the compulsive quid-pro-quo exchange which taints almsgiving at its heart.[16] Hence, for inverted moral reasons, men had come to reserve to themselves, as a kind of spiritual self-preservation, the right to provide for the poor.

Another form of questionable altruism developed into the trend to will one's property to educational or other charities.[17] In such a case, one might be assured of Requiem Masses, as well as the propagation of one's good will through a charity named in the donor's memory.

A resume of the history of hospitals points up the varying fortunes of these centers of poor-relief throughout the medieval era. Under the jurisdiction of nursing orders, their immediate administration depended on the good intent of religious bodies for the fulfillment of their purposes.[18] The ultimate authority of any hospital, however, centered in the office of the local bishop, who claimed jurisdiction over all organizations within his diocese, as well as their properties. For as many tales of financial disorder and moral debauchery as can be posited against the hospitals, an equal number of stories of heroism and excellence can be told. The point at hand merely suggests that the conditions in any hospital depended on the individual administrator, that an insufficient number of hospitals existed, compared with the large number needed, and that no connection existed between one institution and another in order to provide continuing sustenance to the needy in their movements across the land.[19] A case can be made for the position that the medieval administration of poor relief never reached the bulk of the destitute and that any solution whatever to widen needed assistance would have proved of worth.[20]

Down the centuries from the high medieval apex a subtle shift had occurred, from consideration of the need of the recipient to an evaluation of his worthiness as receiver. He came to be judged by whether he was worthy of receiving aid or not, and the threat of its refusal supposedly would frighten the destitute individual into a more righteous state of life.

Begging provided a natural means of support for those who owned no property, a fact accepted unquestioningly throughout the earlier age. Hence, when Vives suggested that begging simply be outlawed, he was attacking a fundamental option of self-support for paupers and of restitution for the wealthy who were working off their personal and social debts. When he went further to suggest that the poor work for the support given them, the Spanish humanist introduced a principle of economics ringing with ominous theological overtones.[21] If the poor were to be paid for their labor, it could be assumed that the work must involve some kind of profit for the original entrepreneur; but this position was contrary to the medieval notion of remuneration for use of capital. In addition, if the poor were to be involved in manufacturing, no matter how simple the process, then the Church should rightfully enter the arena of economics and production in order to supervise ethics. Hence, work took on an essentially personal morality in an area into which the Church had not ventured before.

Even more dangerous an arena for Vives to enter lay in the relations of the mendicant orders to precisely these two points: begging and work in exchange for support. In the twelfth century Francis and Dominic had founded mendicant orders as a protest against the monastic communities that had rigidified social and political life during the preceding years. In the vision of the founders, the friars were to own no property; they were to depend entirely upon the good will of society for their sustenance. However, the intervening years had seen distortions brought into communal life. Individual men of the orders rarely roamed the countryside humbly asking for the simple needs of bread and shelter. Instead, Franciscans and Dominicans had constructed centers in the large cities of Europe. As leading theologians and philosophers in the universities, they wrote and preached on the excellence of almsgiving from the theoretical perspective. However, religious men committed to poverty, yet receiving rich sustenance from their orders, compared cruelly with the growing masses of propertyless men, women, and children, who were thrown literally into the highways of western Europe and into the crowded streets of urban centers ill-prepared to receive them.[22]

Why had this sixteenth century proletariat appeared? Thomas More's answer gives one clue: propertied classes in England had closed their lands to farming and had turned their fields into grazing pastures for sheep. Consequently they were employing fewer hands and were making embarrassingly huge profits on their sale of wool to the new textile industries. In the meantime, weavers, traders, and manufacturers in the cities needed the hands and fingers of workers who flocked to the factories. Employed at substandard wages for inhumanly long hours, laborers could hope for no assistance from outmoded guilds.

Further, monarchs of western Europe continued to recruit men from the land for their armies in a round of self-perpetuating wars. Alliances were so complex that a soldier no longer needed a cause to fight for, merely a commander with orders to follow.

Such an interplay between men and money provided a grossly unfair, but practically effective, means for shattering the last chains of serfdom. Urban and rural poor alike were left without land, tenure, home, and security; their only hope for continued employment rested in duty in the army—or in beggary. Recurring epidemics, slashing soldiers from the army and laborers from the manufacturers' rolls with efficient regularity, allowed for a consistent turnover of men entering into the wandering adult population. It was this large moving mass, evolving into the threatening mobs of the streets and highways, which desperately needed assistance. The radical move to forbid begging by law and substitute employment on public projects as a means of alleviating serious moral, social, and personal evils matched the hopeless existence that sustained pauperism.

Vives's plan casts large power into the hands of local administrators. The individual citizen was only beginning to emerge at that time as a valid social entity; democracy—government by and of the people—was judged anarchy. Aside from the few urban centers, society itself was scattered into isolated communities with little commerce or interest outside local boundaries. Local government was the chief and only level of jurisdiction which reached politically into the lives of ordinary persons. His strategy of placing local administrative responsibilities in municipal authorities capitalized on the existing framework of government. The city's livelihood and welfare could then in fact be settled by executives, such as the senators in Bruges, who could act on their own will and in their own competencies, who could interpret imperial decrees for the locale, and who could thereby buffer the city from undue outside governmental influences. Hence, Vives's basic recommendation—which was to fit comfortably into the political scheme of England—required that the assistance to the poor and distressed should be administered by the secular branch of society. Poor-relief through the Church would supplement that of the state.[23]

ONE CITY'S URBAN STRUCTURE

At the beginning of the sixteenth century the walls of Bruges enclosed a population of about fifty thousand persons, in contrast to Lubeck (20,436), Nuremburg (20,000), Strassburg (26,000), and Cologne (37,000). A network of canals provided full-blown commercial movement within and without the city's districts. Still, indications of the decline to come had already insinuated themselves into contemporary politics and economics.[24]

The river Schets was already showing dangerous signs of sluggishness; a growing level of silt coming up from the sea was sounding the first death knells of a city dependent on trade for existence.[25] Commercial navies consistently chose Antwerp in preference to Bruges. International conferences were held in Bruges with less frequency. Still, the ultimate condition as second-rate center lay at least a century away. Except in the eyes of men who perceived the growing flaws in its structure, Bruges enjoyed a prosperity and reputation identified with wealth and success.

The large population was governed by an integrated series of administrators and civil servants. Presiding over the upper echelon were the senators ("Echevins"), from whom a presiding officer was selected by themselves as burgomaster. Exercising criminal and civil jurisdiction, Senators were elected once a year from among the inhabitants of the city. In their sessions they were attended frequently by a cabinet of councilors, who were also elected from the populace, but served the senators in an advisory capacity. Further, a succession of consultants (pensioners) assisted senators and councilors alike as lawyers and urban officials of varying specialties. Although the members of the permanent body were not paid for their services, but held office in view of their obligations as citizens, pensioners were compensated for their work as the need arose.

The burgomaster performed more tasks than a mere figurehead officer. He assumed leadership in the prosecution of criminal cases. Records show that among his ordinary duties he had unlimited rights of arrest, and he personally assigned all suits and disputes involving injuries to a lower level of settlement when he did not preside over the litigation himself. At night he apparently had the duty to visit taverns and houses of ill repute in order to oversee the maintenance of order.

A bank of lower officials carried out the legislative acts passed by the senators. Employed by the city, they provided for smooth maintenance of urban services in a city whose base population frequently swelled or diminished by the movement of foreigners in trade and specialized industries. For the sick, two physicians, eight midwives, and two surgeons formed a regular panel of available assistance. The latter were authorized to increase their number during a plague. Two treasurers, who supervised the flow of city moneys, also acted as legal officers in their right to inspect buildings for safety and to compensate owners for property confiscated by city fiat, as when the city decreed the widening of streets and canals.

The city had been divided into six sections, each able to isolate itself from the others through an ingenious system of gates and dams. Six captains played the roles of executives of the divisions, and had charge of the keys as virtual and actual commandants of the areas.

Supervisors of street conditions figured as city employees. However, city services did not include street lighting, which was left to private enterprise. If necessary, individual householders would provide torches outside their dwellings. Generally, citizens as a matter of personal safety rarely traveled at night through the city.

A force of officers of the peace consisted of policemen and watchmen, who kept public and domestic peace, with the rights of arrest granted them. Firemen employed by the city organized the volunteers of each district; centers were established for equipment, including buckets and other appliances. A follow-up on the causes of fires was conducted by the equivalent of an arson squad, with appropriate penalties for discovered guilt.

Scavengers comprised one of the most important bodies of officials. Appointed to remove mud and filth from the streets and canals, they were by law to keep public places clean and trim. Assisting them, a crew of dogcatchers regularly hunted out the animals whose consistent crime lay in snatching bread and edible products from the markets and displays. Considered a serious public nuisance, they were simply exterminated as indicated, for example, by the records of 1486 to 1490, when 4,356 dogs were eliminated on official count.

Before 1556, the senators and councilors of Bruges left poor relief primarily to the various private associations of religious and parish origins, but occasionally interfered in the interest of efficiency rather than principle. Vives refers to the senate action in 1512, which developed a trade school for boys out of a center for beggars, but generally the separation between civic and religious organizations was clearly distinct.

The demarcation was hazier in cities like Brussels and Louvain, where control of institutional poor relief had passed to municipal authorities through appointment of lay trustees over private charities. In theory the cities administered the programs but in fact the actual administration of remedial services remained in the hands of the religious bodies, such as sisterhoods and nursing communities, which divided the responsibility and resulted in ineffectiveness on both sides.

Vives designed his pattern for poor relief in Bruges specifically for his own city, yet he included the principle of municipal administration applicable anywhere. Apparently the city of Lille adopted his plan of action in 1527, Ypres (with modifications) in 1529, and Mons, Oudendarde, and Valenciennes in 1531.[26] His principles appear in the Imperial Decree of Charles V for the Empire in 1531 and, according to the thesis of this paper, in the first systematic poor law of England promulgated by Henry VIII in 1531.

The irony of Bruges's refusal to amend its poor-relief system until 1556[27] reflects not the needs of the city nor the apparent goodwill of the men who requested Vives to study their city, but rather the religious revolution raging on every front of human endeavor during the intervening years. As a matter of record, Bruges adapted its administration only in 1556, after the bitterness of controversy over Protestant directions had fractured the unity of Christian churches and the Council of Trent had condemned the use of civil authorities as primary administrators in the relief of the poor.[28]

THE AUTHOR WITHIN HIMSELF

Juan Luis Vives had first gone to England with the sole intent of stopping over on his journey to Spain in May 1523.[29] However, as Cardinal Wolsey engaged him as a lecturer in the newly formed Cardinal College, housed at Corpus Christi, Oxford, the Spanish humanist remained until the spring of the next year. A second stay at Oxford began the following October (1524) and continued to the following April (1525), during which time Vives continued to give his lectures on the classics.

In the meantime, he had entered a circle of English luminaries in letters and politics. Frequently a guest at the court of Henry and Catherine and a visitor in the homes of prominent men, Vives had become acquainted with Thomas Linacre, William Latimer, Thomas Elyot, Cuthbert Tunstall, John Longland, Thomas Lupset, and John Fisher. Thomas More had been introduced to him three years earlier in Bruges by Francis Craneveldt, their mutual friend, and the English humanist had immediately brought the Spanish erudite into a sphere of subtle political influence. It was through More that Wolsey was persuaded to ask Vives to be lecturer in the first place; it was through More that the Queen negotiated for her fellow countryman some minor gratuities which made his livelihood a little less precarious.

During April 1525 Vives stayed with the More family, where he came to know those astounding English women whom he was later to eulogize in his essay on female education. It was there that he probably met Richard Hyrde, whose introduction to the English translation of *Education of a Christian Woman* reveals a modern intuition in pedagogy. That month in the home of the English lawyer, politician, author, and associate of kings and chancellors provided hours of "merry" conversation for the two humanists, whether alone or with the numerous visitors who seemed permanent features of the More menage. Among the latter were two administrators from the Lowlands, one the president of Great Parliament at Mechlin, and the other a former burgomaster of the Senate of Bruges.

Josse Lauwereyns[30] held the prestigious position of presiding officer over the chief court of justice for the northern Imperial provinces. He was currently on a mission as an Imperial negotiator with Admiral Asolph of Beveren and Johan de la Sanche between February and June 1525. Questions have been consistently raised about the relationship that may have existed between Vives and the Councilors of Ypres who in September of that year (1525) instituted an innovative program of poor-relief reform and in December published an outline of its content.[31] The intriguing query tantalizes: how much influence did Vives and Ypres exert on each other? No records have been found to confirm any direct contact between the city to the south and the Spaniard already widely known for his attitudes about contemporary social problems of peace, international obligations, and human rights in general. Vives may easily have journeyed to Ypres without leaving traces; councilors or advisers may have been among his listeners in the Halles at the University in Louvain; some may have been in residence in his guest house for students and travelers in Louvain, to which he invited paying guests to supplement a meager income.

However, his meeting with Lauwereyns while both were in London in the spring of 1525 may provide the connection between the Ypres and Bruges plans for poor relief. As a man in charge of the province-wide administration of justice, frequently concerned with its application toward beggars and breakers of the law—the latter, more from hungry desperation than from malicious insubordination—Lauwereyns must have questioned the Spanish humanist on the conflicts between poverty and society. Perhaps through their discussions the men of Ypres received the large concepts which in their work so clearly resemble the work of Juan Luis Vives.

A second man of politics, Louis de Praet,[32] either directly inspired Vives to write *On Assistance to the Poor* or at least encouraged its composition. Like the president of the Great Parliament, he was a native of Bruges. He had been in England from May 1522 until that same month in 1525. Vives refers to him in the dedicatory preface:

Actually I had been asked to do this some time ago, when I was in England, by Lord Praet, your Burgomaster, who deliberates deeply and often—as indeed he ought—concerning the public welfare of the city.

Conditions in London were not so different from those in Bruges. Perhaps that April the similar deprivations in two similar centers of population brought these men of the Brabant to lament the deplorable situation, and the one to plot a strategy of relief.

However, a third and obvious influence permeated those days, Thomas More himself. He had written a fable almost ten years before, a fable not so subtle but that its impact of blame and censure was clearly felt on sensitive government levels.[33] Poverty was not meant to scar the landscape of Utopia; More's immediate solution was to withdraw the misused rights of wealthy landowners who had turned their land from crops to grazing fields through enclosures. In those intervening years, as a matter of record, the number of poor and destitute who crowded into English cities and peopled the highways had grown phenomenally. Still, More did not attempt to remedy the immediate condition through any scheme of public assistance. Surely More and Vives must have spent no little time on the practicalities of poverty; the need to outlaw begging in fact, as well as in letters; the means of determining who were the poor in order to distribute the goods of the city with greater justice; and the urgency of education for the children of the poor because without education the future itself boded ill for the state. While he did not actually write his essay on poor relief while in England, it demands too much of the imagination—and of a sensitivity about both More and Vives—to assume that they had never discussed the concept at some length.

During the last six months of 1525 Vives's frequent correspondence with Francis Craneveldt plumbed his hopes and fears for the new work. Perhaps because of his conversations with Lauwereyns or some unknown contact with Ypres, he was most reluctant to let even his closest associates know what his current writing included. Thus, on June 20, 1525, he noted:

I have projected a certain work with such conclusions that I do not dare disclose them to you because you will judge me to have gone mad.[34]

On September 17 he wrote:

I assert that my fetus is a tardy little matter; truly it will emerge rapidly enough if it emerges at all. No one satisfies me as midwife except Christ. I am imploring His divine will and power; otherwise, it would be ejected stillborn and without life.[35]

A month later, in answer to Craneveldt's questions demanding some kind of satisfying answers to his enigmatical evasions, he wrote:

I would explain to you the title and structure of the book verbally in the presence of all, but I do not dare entrust them to a letter, even to a dearest friend, for fear that it would fall into wrong hands. I'll not bring my idea forth sooner than the elephant, providing I don't abort, but not with the nine-year gestation as the common people think, but the two-year period as the naturalists teach us.[36]

He was close to finishing the work in December; but even before it had been completed, Craneveldt had ferreted out some hint of its content. In commenting on these estimates, Vives conceded:

What you tell me that finally you have managed to scent out—which I hid so scrupulously even from so great a friend—is indeed that first part of the work. For my part, I would not divulge more to you if you were present than to Ruffault, my young friend at hand.[37]

The fact that he was so liberal in discussing his other works as they progressed indicates that an unusual restraint was placed on him. Was it some agreement between him and the Ypres councilors? Or was it some fear that the theologians would get wind of his ideas and condemn them before they were published?

At any rate, after the book had been published at the end of March 1526, Vives penned a letter to Craneveldt on April 13 and spoke freely, perhaps because he was then at Oxford:

I don't know if you have read my little book, "On Assistance to the Poor," as presented in Bruges, plagued with errors though it is. What an amateur printer! Read it, please, and send me as soon as possible your reactions, annotating as you are accustomed to do. . . . In my affairs I am sailing ahead with only adverse currents. But I hope that I can navigate out of this situation because good wind is beginning to blow. No other thing do I desire more than home, quiet, and hearth, in order to finish the large amount of work begun and to polish rough edges. If it seems to you that in "On Assistance to the Poor" there is something which is suitable for the Province, please inform those who can help and promote the work.[38]

Worrying about the legal basis for his humanistic recommendations, he asked in June:

I should like to know from you what the laws seem like for the succor of the poor. This worries me more than all of prosody and the fine points of grammar.[39]

Four years later the faculties of the Sorbonne were to condemn the Ypres plan on the basis of its then heretical principle of reassigning the administration of poor relief from religious groups to the secular arm of the government.[40] Vives anticipated this move, for he noted in a letter of October 1, 1527:

Unless my eyes deceive me, I do not see any place in the book where it contains heresy or the calumny of a "most imprudent" man, even for unjust inquisitors. Into this I put special care, that there would be nothing to mar the fruit which I proposed to produce and by which I would reach out to many thousands of mortals.[41]

His fear of interference from the strong clerical bloc in the faculties at the University of Louvain, let alone the more distant colleges of Paris, seems justified in the rapid reaction to his essay. The Bishop of Sarepta openly condemned it as heretical, resembling a subversive threat to the ecclesiastical status quo, and—most damaging judgment for the times—obviously a product of the Lutheran sect.

Herbert de Crooc's edition exhibited misprints on almost every page, but the book itself was in immediate demand everywhere. Within two months the printer had issued a second edition, supposedly corrected by the author but still suffering from typographical errors. Within five years translations appeared in French, Spanish, and Italian. No English translation was published, perhaps because the men who were to write the Poor Laws of 1531 and 1536 knew its content in the Latin original. It was only in 1535, for the sake of the nonspecialists, that Thomas Marshall translated the document on poor-relief as published by the Council of Ypres.[43]

What elements contributed to the making of a mind at once perceptive of the past and effectively projective for the future? Undoubtedly, Vives's own amiable yet complex personality,[44] his early years in the Spain of Moors, Jews, and Christians, and his humanism come lately after the first grounding in Aristotelianism[45] had readied his mind for the creation of alternatives.

In the year of his birth (1492), the city of Valencia rested on an apex of past glories and future decline.[46] Mentioned by Livy, Roman settlers under Junius Brutus brought the *jus Latinum* to Valencia in 138 B.C. Pompey conquered its walls and partially destroyed the town in 75 B.C., and then called for its reinstatement as a colony. From then on, the predatory urge of Mediterranean conquerors caught up the settlement in a series of foreign cultures, each entering intimately into the land and its peoples. In 413 A.D. the Visigoths took Valencia; then in 714 the Moors had their turn. After the downfall of Cordova in 1021 A.D. the town and its surrounding dependencies were created into a Caliphate. The brash, romantic fling of the Cid brought Valencia its freedom in 1094, but only briefly until it was retaken by the Moors in 1101.

Arab victors allowed, indeed demanded, that defeated nations assume their own self-government. Hence, the Kingdom of Valencia was re-established in 1146. However, Spanish administrators forced Valencia to become a tributary to Aragon in 1172; eventually it was added to the domains of James I of Aragon in 1238 and, finally, in 1500, just after Vives's birth, it was annexed to Castille and placed under a viceroy of Ferdinand and Isabella's joint government.

Each large event in the life of the city left a mark of the conquerors, generally in the administration of government and, specifically, in the manner and means of assisting segments of the population disadvantaged through race, poverty, illness, or misfortune. For example, under the Moors the Cortes of Aragon had extensive powers for investigating injustices, whether these came from the king, his officers, or merely a man's neighbor.[47]

In 1337 Valencia made special provisions for the protection of orphans by means of the appointment of an official to do that duty, which in time was extended to authority over all minors who needed the protection of the law.[48] Throughout the Caliphates, taxes imposed on perishable goods were assigned directly to the relief of the poor. Such products made up the basic Valencian diet: olives, grapes, figs, apples, six kinds of melon, pears, pomegranates, oranges, lemons, bananas, dates (these specifically imported because the climate in Valencia near the sea was not dry enough), peaches, almonds, quinces, and chestnuts.[49] Further, a considerable portion of public revenue was expended on the development of needed communal facilities and public utilities, as well as poor relief proper. Al-Hakan II spent lavishly on building projects such as mosques, baths, inns, markets, and fountains. More significantly, some of the construction included houses for the destitute, hospitals for the indigent ill, schools for the poor. Before the end of the Moorish rule every town had its public hospital, while well-to-do Muslim and Jewish physicians rendered free medical services to the poor.[50]

One Moorish engineering feat still functions in Valencia to this day, a system of irrigation canals, ditches, and flumes which spreads out from the city to its western mountains. A veritable paradise of lush vegetation in its natural state, the Huerta grew immeasureably more productive when irrigation no longer depended on seasonal rainfall and untrained waterways, but became obedient to the command of engineers and administrators.[51] Where one crop had been raised, now there were three; agriculture was now beholden to man and his decisions, decisions made by the Water Tribunal every Thursday at noon outside the Apostles' Door of the cathedral. The Moors had established this council of growers and townsmen alike, who would make the decision about which area should be watered, and at what time the waters would pass through a man's property. A man could petition for more water, protest its cost, or complain against his neighbor's unjust diversion of the flow.

This was the Valencia into which Vives was born,[52] a city well-administered for over a thousand years by "secular" authorities. This orientation formed his consciousness from his earliest years, as opposed to the imputed motivation of dispensing with ecclesiastical control in the distribution of assistance to the poor. In his early experience, he knew no other mode of efficient poor relief except the secular.

Still other influences on the mind of the Spanish humanist originate in the heritage that both he and his city claimed from the Jews of Valencia. When the Moors selected administrators for civic enterprises throughout Spain, their choice was as often a Jew as a Christian. The records of this early-day "ecumenism" indicate that violence and persecution for religious reasons rarely characterized the relations between or among the three religious bodies. Only with Ferdinand and Isabella's Inquisition supporting the expulsion orders for non-Christians, mounting in violence yearly, did the acceptance of Jews as administrators come undone. The "Golden Age" of Jews in Spain spanned the eleventh and twelfth centures;[53] in contrast, the tragedy of persecution grew simultaneously with the strength of the Christian Church until by 1500 they were finally an exiled, hunted people. Until then, Spanish Jews had contributed richly to local and provincial government through their technical acuity and economic aid.

Juan Luis Vives himself belonged to a strong stock of Hispanic Jews.[54] Though baptized as an infant, he attended a synagogue school until he was ten years of age. While records remain scanty, it can be deduced that the older Juan Luis and his mother, Blanche Marche, of whom the loyal son wrote so affectionately in later years, willed for him education in the Christian religion and acculturation in the life and ideals of Judaism. The boy fell heir to the optimism of authentic Christianity and the pessimism of a people who must always be ready for persecution. In Jewish literature and philosophy the world of the inner self offers a greater challenge to study than the rationale of rejection by Christians. Like other men of Jewish extraction before and after him, he was so aware of his own inner life that he could disengage himself from an object-oriented philosophy. He concentrated on man's relations with other men—whether in education, philosophy, morality, poor relief, law, and letters—in order to ask the radical questions: Who is man? Why is man? Why does he opt so often for war, hatred, and cruelty? So Vives turned to treatises on pedagogy, peace, the classics, and the practical means of assisting the nation through assistance to the poor.[55]

Jews had resided too long in Spain to remain detached from Moslem thinking. The depths of this man of Valencia reveal a hidden interaction of thought among Moslem, Jewish, and Christian origins. No one of these influences is significant alone; rather, it is from their interfacings that the distinctive Hispanic culture derives. Out of this has come a certain spiritual "modality," expressed on the one hand as illuminism, mysticism, or the Erasmianism of the sixteenth century, and on the other hand as a holy joyousness responding to the heady environment of color and romance, through pastorals and picaresque narratives.

In such a triune vision, man is an energetic, "shifting, changeable reality," rather than a being conceived in metaphysical categories and distant abstractions. Man creates himself as a reality moment by moment. Almost a thousand years ago, Abn-Hazm had said that "the essence of man is to be found in immanent motivation."[56] The humanists of northern Europe held themselves intent on the task of defining man in terms of freedom and essence; but the years in Valencia allowed Vives to define man as a creature living precariously in a world of experience and joined in society with men by intimate, yet fragile, bonds.[57] So, for example, as he wrote his propaganda essays favoring peace, Vives involved the reader and himself deeply in his choice to leave the fatherland rather than accept war as a way of life. He would recount the "sad reality that both the public and private morals of Christians are too often evil and corrupt, and those of the impious sound and laudable." He went on to say: "We profess the law of Christ but do not practice it."[58] Rather than create a new religion, he chose the more painful option of remaining within the Church. Firmly, probably fearfully, he proposed social organizations that would resolve the contradiction between the affluence of wealthy Christians and the indigence of men "who never heard a sermon or took part in the Lord's Supper."

The contrast with his humanist friends darkens in such dimensions. Thomas More prescribed the elimination of the current landholding system with no bread-and-butter proposals for the immediate condition of the poor. Erasmus longed for a society resembling the early Church without making adjustments for the new age of technology, science, and brute economics already influential in the Europe of the 1520s. Vives was at one with the poverty of his times, probably because he had himself suffered its privations and its imprisonment for debt. The awareness of his own private agonies led him to put aside abstract reasoning and consider fundamental issues. He never arrived at irrevocable solutions for society's quandaries. More than other thinkers, he labored toward an idealized integration of body and soul, reality and theory, philosophy and theology. He was always conscious of the tensions existing between the inner and the outer. His path was not a direct march down the via media, but rather a personal journey between two extremes of radicalism. Acting with an existential wisdom and perceptive prudence, he rose from his own life of pain and joy to speak tentatively to other men.

Ever and always a Spaniard, Vives accepted the influences of his past and present to produce a unique response to a northern European environment. Innovation for its own sake—innovation which was merely external to the problem—denied an authenticity of the life that filled his vision. The new for him was an extension of the immanent; it signified growth from within, emerging out of the natural condition of men and their times. Hence, his innovative recommendations for social reform simply emerge as existential solutions for Bruges, with practical adaptations possible in Louvain or Ypres or London. Each of his procedures—the basic analysis of poverty, the census of the poor, the control of moneys in order to offset pilfering, the right of the poor to work and the correlative duty of the state to provide employment, the development of public works through a judicious use of the otherwise unemployed, the sensitivity that administrators must express in their personal relationships with the impoverished—all these indicate a distinctive personalism and individualism which is Vives's mentality, stemming as it does from a unique Spanish-Moorish-Jewish origin.

The Hispanic Jew and the Hispanic Moslem tradition saw man as a vital, shifting existant.[59] Vives absorbed the desperation of the real. The absence of peace had led him to "anguished meditation" on the inner reality that could create such horrors. It brought him to proposals for social action which would relieve man's needs immediately. Regretfully, when English poor laws were first formulated, they took on the pragmatic solution without its mystical counterpart, perhaps opening the way to a "social welfare" disconnected from sympathy and understanding in the face of destitution and suffering.

THE ENGLISH LINK

The literature of English poor laws, comprehensive and detailed as it is, requires only a cursory summary here as a useful perspective. A brief review confirms the effectiveness of the Poor Laws as a *modus vivendi* intimately affecting class structure, early capitalism, developing mercantilism, and labor relations generally.

Records from 1430 disclose a series of laws dealing with the indigent and unemployed laborers. Statutes in the 1530s carry the same objectives of relief and the same means of administration through the parish. However, two new theories had appeared: one, that it was the duty of the state, not the Church, to provide for the poor; and, second, that begging as a means of support for the indigent and unhoused was to be outlawed.

John Major had developed the rationale behind the first notion in his commentaries on the *Sentences* of Peter Lombard.[60] Pamphlets such as *A*

Supplication for the Beggers (1529), by Simon Fish, *A Supplication to our most Sovereign Lord King Henry the Eighth* (1544), *A Supplication on the Poor Commons* (1546), and *The Decaye of England* (1550-53) indicate the popular interest expressed by a local intelligentsia roused against the clergy, the traditional administrators of relief to the poor.[61]

Concerning the second principle newly entering into Tudor thinking, important cities in the Germanies had already passed statutes forbidding begging within their boundaries. Ridley was only one of several eloquent preachers who urged this concept on Edward VI, while others throughout the important parishes of the country proposed the same action.[62]

Both principles are essential to Vives's overall development of relief measures. His close association with the English king in the happier days before Henry's divorce and Wolsey's manhandling of the Spanish humanist unquestionably influenced subsequent legislation. Henry delighted in working with his men from Parliament; the statute of 1531 breathes the person of the English monarch attempting to be as contemporary in social concerns as any of the continental senates and councils.[63] It would require seventy years of Tudor administration, seventy years of lean living for the poor of England, before the great Elizabethan law finally coordinated the myriad statutes of the previous decades into the dramatic document of 1601. Throughout the growth and development of this corpus of laws the recurring principles give testimony to the influence of *On Assistance to the Poor.*[64]

According to the act of 1531 magistrates were to record the names of the poor. A license was required for begging, a move prerequisite to the ultimate total restriction on mendicancy. So intrinsic to the economic system, the ban on begging threatened to remove the platform under fiscal welfare of the nation as a whole.[65] The phasing-out period, linked to a progressive program of substitute assistance, would have been essential to the common welfare.

With the act of 1536 provisions were made for the impotent poor, that is, those without any means whatever for assisting themselves. The parish was to take over poor relief from the monasteries, which were already under condemnation proceedings. Henceforth, the parish was to provide for immediate assistance[66] and eventual employment by which the poor were to support themselves. Coordinated efforts to provide for labor on public works had not yet emerged, although some conversations on the matter began during the period; for example, the townsmen of Dover requested such assistance during a series of damaging floods.[67] The law further provided that parishioners were to receive a most serious exhortation from their pastors and select laymen in regard to almsgiving, and the person who refused was suspect of ill-will or even religious unorthodoxy. A "common box" was to be established within the parish for the collection of moneys for the poor so that an equitable distribution might be made to all the poor throughout the parish, rather than to the donor's preferred few.

Acts under Edward VI introduced three strategies. The first—with sections forcing "sturdy beggars" into slavery, branding them with an S, demanding the death penalty for run-aways, and proposing regulations for apprentices—was soon repealed as too stringent, but organizational control tightened in subsequent measures. The method of taking a census, as specified by Vives, was adopted. In the cities and towns, the mayor—and in the country, the parson or churchwarden—was to provide the statistics of the poor of the district and to maintain the records ready for inspection at all times. Two men named as "collectors" were to take pledges of alms from the self-supporting citizenry. Were the parishioner reluctant to contribute a share, he was then obliged to appear before the bishop, a threatening confrontation for the 1540s and 1550s.

Finally, an attempt was made at housing, whereby a cottage should be made available for the helpless, nonresident poor within each locality. Simultaneously, these poor were to take up employment immediately or else move on to their own parishes. Penalties for begging followed a consistent pattern of cruelty, which was nevertheless accepted passively by a people hardened to the cruelty of mere existence.

Statutes under Mary and Philip confirmed the legislation of Henry, rather than of Edward, with little change. A weekly collection was to be made in the parishes. Begging continued to be forbidden. Under this regime the destitute could be given passports to the continent in their search for support.

During Elizabeth's first year as Queen, Mary's statutes were confirmed; but from then on the tangible growth and legal coordination of poor laws took on impetus. In 1562-63 persons refusing to contribute to parish alms were to be assessed, even to the point of having their property held, subject to the needful relief of the destitute. Employment was obligatory upon everyone of an age or ability to work, while justices of the peace were assigned the right to fix the rate of wages.

The year 1572 brought an entirely new approach: the former statutes were completely repealed. Now beggars were to be severely punished; those refusing to work were to be chastised; and persons harboring or relieving such individuals—still called "sturdy beggars"—were themselves subject to penalties. The aged and infirm were to have specific places to which they were assigned, whether in their own parishes or not, in order to clear the highways of some of the traffic which seriously threatened the well-being of travelers.[68] If by some chance extra money after alms accrued, it was to be given to those poor who were working, with the proviso that it be applied to their living necessities. In other words, provision for relief supplemented employment wages, a new strategy of relief. Four years later, a statute developed these aspects further. Work was to be provided for the poor (such as weaving, a typical occupation of the time); materials necessary for such manufacturing would be provided by means of taxation on the local inhabitants. In turn, the products thus made by the poor were to be sold, with profits being added to the fund for the same purpose. "Houses of correction" were to be established, in which both work and punishment were provided for the unemployed destitute. "Censors" and "wardens" were to be appointed to provide some semblance of morality and order.

Because these measures approached the problem realistically and somewhat centrally, they sufficed until the next large development in 1597-98. The "collectors" of Edward's time became the "overseers" appointed in every parish. It also became possible to tax a wealthier parish for the support of one less well-financed. The notion of the mutual liability of parents and children for support throughout their lives entered the system at this juncture. Hospitals, houses of correction, and "abiding places" for the elderly and ill were now to be erected only under government license.

By the end of her reign, Elizabeth's legislators had integrated and organized the many scattered parts of poor legislation into a document whose influence was transported to the American colonies a few years later. In addition to codifying all the earlier elements, it recognized that punishment alone was not an answer to dire and immediate need; hence, public relief was to be undertaken as a responsibility of the state and was to be underwritten by public support. This assistance to the poor was seen as a security for life and property, as well as an assurance of the due ascendancy of the law.

Still, Elizabeth's program did not attack the institution of poverty. Society's obligation ended at public assistance. The state in the next years was to assume economic leadership through a mercantilist political theory. It became a totalitarian directing agency, setting prices, fixing wages, determining apprenticeship standards, chartering stock companies, and granting patents for land. In this inheritance the American colonies came into existence and began to create their Americanized version of the English relief system—almshouses for "honest poor," workhouses for idlers, prisons for vagabonds, public hospitals for ill paupers, all with assistance from private and religious charities.[69]

AMERICAN COUNTERPART

Whether in Plymouth or Virginia, the first colonists arrived from England ready to establish a plantation of hope for themselves and their posterity. However, their intellectual heritage and ethical orientation decided for them and succeeding generations that any "new" format of government and society would be only a variation on English law and custom. When the colonies were founded, the procedures for dealing with the poor had already been functioning in the homeland for over half a century. Hence, it is not surprising to find a colonial development of Elizabeth's legislation operating in the same direction, with the pace restrained and little enlargement of principles. Essays, analyses, and original archival sources prove that the Elizabethan Poor Law of 1601 received little original application in the colonies. Rather, it served as a model in fact and in spirit for American adaptations from their earliest passage even to the twentieth century. When formulating their own legislation, the original seaboard colonies imitated the laws from England. In turn, the states in the Ohio Valley, and then beyond the Mississippi, duplicated the colonial patterns in terminology and purpose, as can be noted by even the most general survey of the competent and large literature available.[70]

In New England, the first general laws concerned the impotent poor. Thus, Plymouth Colony decreed in 1642 that every town should maintain the poor "according as they shall fynd moar convenyent and suitable for themselves by an order and general agreement in a publike town meeting."[71] Very much like the educational law passed that year, the responsibility of relief to the indigent was introduced with both positive and negative results. The actual formulation of a set of procedures for poor relief originated in Connecticut in 1673, for this reason designated as the first "real poor law" of New England. It provided that after three-months' residence, any person who "by sickness, lameness or the like comes to want" should be assisted by that town.[72]

As the needs and the colonies grew, Pennsylvania organized its assistance through law in 1688, and Massachusetts in 1692. The growing populations of smaller towns in the latter colony manifested a reluctance to assume their civic burden; by various means they funneled large numbers of the indigent poor into the city of Boston. Costs for poor relief there doubled between 1728 and 1734, as noted in one request for larger grants from the governor's office. In the nearby town of Braintree, almost 36 percent of the city's total expenditure was poured into poor relief.

The task of differentiating between the "impotent poor" and the "sturdy beggars" was unduly problematic to New England councilmen.[73] In spite of strong Calvinistic legislation that no idler be allowed among the diligent laborers of the colony, laziness and vagabondry festered in the growing community. In 1682 Massachusetts passed laws forbidding idling, even to the extent of providing for visitors who would enter the homes of suspected dawdlers and report deviation to constables.

Connecticut moved to correct this defect in capable adult men by its legislation of 1713.[74] Further, it began to turn from "putting out" in private homes—an adaptation for providing shelter for the poor without constructing buildings for the purpose—to the erection of public almshouses, houses of corrections, and common jails for debtors and offenders.

In Virginia, poor relief was expectedly centered around the organization of the parish system.[75] In 1634 counties were created; and in 1641 these were divided into parishes. Freeholders elected the twelve-man governing board of the parish. Beginning in 1646 and continuing to 1769, at least eight series of laws concerning the care of the children of the poor were enacted. The unique condition of Virginia's development explains the consistent emphasis on assistance to youth: the presence of indentured servants (sometimes the vagabonds and paupers of England pressed into colonial service), men and women not indentured but employed as servants, slaves free or bound, a growing number of mullatos—all these predicted large numbers of children born to penury and ignorance.

The vestrymen prepared a budget based on the needs forseeable for the year and then tithed the members of the parish equally. One means of poor relief required the placement of the impoverished individual in the home of a wealthy parishioner; in other cases, direct relief in kind and in money was provided the indigent on a temporary basis in order to allow recouping of health or finances lost by accidents or unforeseen exigencies.

As the counties increased in number and the population grew in size, the parishes accordingly lost their effectiveness as centers of poor relief. Hence, in 1785, after a series of acts preparing for the action, the administration of relief was removed from the vestrymen and placed in the office of the county "overseer." This action led finally to a separation of church and state in Virginia at the beginning of the constitutional era of the nation.

Obviously, then, leadership and patterning in poor relief came from Massachusetts, Connecticut, and Pennsylvania. As the Northwest Territory opened, and statutes were devised, first by territories and then by states as they advanced toward organized sociopolitical units, western legislators simply imitated—indeed, plagiarized—the phrasing and the intent of the old colonial laws for assisting the poor. One researcher categorically states,

> The poor laws which are found on the statute books of our forty-eight states are most of them survivals of the statutes adopted more than a century ago in one state after another, patterned after the old colonial laws, which in the beginning had followed the general principles of the English poor law as it was finally formulated in the so-called "great poor law" at the close of the Elizabethan period in 1601.[76]

For example, in 1790 a legislative assembly meeting in Marietta, Ohio, wrote into law the obligation of public support of the indigent and authorized the county justices to appoint overseers for the administration of funds. In turn, a local justice of the peace was to be responsible for dealing directly with the specific needs of individuals.[77] The principle was incorporated into the early constitutions of Kansas (1859), Nevada (1864), North and South Dakota (1895), South Carolina (1895), and Oklahoma (1907). Similarly, reflections of the same principle can be observed in growth to maturity from the early constitution of the state of Illinois (1819), with a continuing supplement by statute to 1874, retained to 1970, albeit with the addition of innumerable amendments.[78]

The elements of American poor relief, which historically—and, in some variations, even presently—originate in the Elizabethan laws, can be epitomized as:

1. the responsibility of the state for the relief of the poor;
2. the right to levy taxes on the body politic in order to provide for the less fortunate and the dependent;
3. the responsibility of the local community for the poor within their confines;
4. the creation of special offices in order to forward the actual administration of the program;
5. a differentiation among the varieties of poor;
6. workhouses for the able-bodied poor, or the provision of work for the

poor and the materials and equipment necessary for their employment.

Documents are not wanting to illustrate these elements.[79] As in 1601, these adaptations of the Elizabethan law—no matter how enlightened the more recent may appear—accept the institution of poverty as an irremedial fact whose existence must be assumed to be perpetual, whose presence must be acknowledged as indisputable and unchanging.[80]

The astounding fact remains that for over three hundred years American assistance to the poor has retained a format of assistance appropriate to the rural life of England under the Tudors,[81] but perceptively more dysfunctional as the nation has grown into the technological, industrial complex of the late twentieth century. The elimination of poverty in a cybernetic society is no longer available to the initiative or motivation of the individual, for too often he is caught up helplessly in the web of national transportation, geographical mobility, instant communication, and global distribution of goods and services—all beyond his personal control.

In retrospect, assistance to the poor points to developmental stages in the evolution of man in his imperfect society.[82] In the earliest Christian communities, almsgiving was an act originating in the virtue of charity without concern for the recipient. As time progressed, the emphasis shifted to the need of the recipient, rather than the desire of the donors; and so bequests were instituted for schools and hospitals. Beginning with Vives and evolving over the past three centuries, efforts began to focus on a common plan for national or state administration, as opposed to the well-intentioned but ineffective isolated, local efforts. Now, nations have arrived at a fourth phase, concerned not so much with individuals as with given segments of the population served through the coordinated efforts of private and public resources (as opposed to the distinctly individualized philanthropy of either). Thus, contemporary thrusts focus on maternity centers, health clinics, child centers for working mothers, homes for unwed mothers, employment training centers, schools for the mentally retarded, the blind, and the deaf, day care or total custody for the mentally disturbed—and more.

Historically, relief to the poor functions most effectively when its administration reflects the social and political format of the age in which it operates; this fact is observable when the origin of assistance is the local ecclesia, monastery, parish, overseer's office, city, senate, or modern social security administration. The question then appropriately arises: what is the most effective means of assistance to the poor in the 1970s? Do present modes resemble the mobile, isolated, technologically oriented society of these latter years of the twentieth century? or do they take on the regal, paternalistic, localized thrust of a Tudor era four hundred years distant and hence fail to fulfill the needs of desperate citizens locked into poverty and dependence? Vives knew the risks he took with his radical propositions; his history may assist in the predictions of poor-relief for the next forty, if not four hundred, years.

Whatever the next development, it must inevitably move from the merely national to the international level. To paraphrase a contemporary phrase-maker, the world is a global parish. The obligation of the wealthy nations to assist the less fortunate can surely be no less binding today than it was in 1526 for Vives, who insisted that the well-to-do parishes should assist the needy ones of Bruges. The radicalism of the sixteenth-century humanist challenges the present era to an equally ingenious commitment to social values outlawing, not begging, but poverty itself throughout the world.

PART II

ON ASSISTANCE TO THE POOR

by

Juan Luis Vives

translated by

Sister Alice Tobriner

PREFACE

To the Councilors and the Senate of Bruges—

Cicero says that it is a duty of travelers and visitors to avoid overcuriosity when abroad in a foreign state. He is right, for prying into the affairs of others can be despicable. However, concern and friendly advice will probably not be rejected because the law of nature holds that anything human is not extraneous to man, simply because it is human. Further, the grace of Christ, like a cohesive glue, has cemented all men to each other.

Although I am to a certain degree an alien here myself, I am as truly bound to this city as I am to my own Valencia. I do not call Bruges anything other than homeland, for I have lived here for fourteen years (even if not continuously), and I always return here as to my very home. I delight in your administrative system, the education and civility of your citizens, the extraordinary tranquility and justice which pervade the city and are renowned throughout the world.

For these reasons I married here. I deeply desire your well-being. I am determined to remain in this city and no other for whatever length of my life Christ may graciously grant to me. I consider myself a citizen of this city, and toward its residents I have the same mind as toward my own brothers.

The extreme poverty of so many of them compels me to write how I think they might be assisted. Actually, I had been asked to do this some time ago, when I was in England, by Lord Praet, your burgomaster, who deliberates deeply and often—as, indeed, he ought—concerning the public welfare of the city.

I dedicate this work to you, first, because you are completely committed to benevolence and to the relief of the poor, as confirmed by the crowds of poor who surge to you as to a refuge already prepared for them; secondly, because cities originate where, relief being given and received, love takes root in mutual assistance and strengthens itself through the fellowship of men. There, administrators of the city strive to insure that each man assists others, that no one is oppressed, that no one is wronged by an unjust condemnation, and that the strong assist the weak. Thus, the peace of an entire and united citizenry grows in love each day and endures.

Just as it is disgraceful for the head of a household to allow any member to suffer the lack of food or the embarrassment of wandering in rags, so it follows that, in a wealthy city, its magistrates would not permit its citizens—even a few—to be pressed down by undue hunger and misery.

May it please you to read this. If it does not please you, at least consider the matter most carefully, just as you would investigate with great diligence the litigation of a private person in which a large sum of money is disputed.

May all prosperity and good fortune attend you and this city!

VIVES

Bruges, January 6, 1526

I

THE OBLIGATIONS OF ADMINISTRATORS
IN A CITY TOWARD THE POOR

My references here are to the state and the administrator, who is to the former as a soul is to the body. The soul quickens and animates not merely this or that part, but the entire body; thus, the magistrate may never disregard a portion of his governance.

Those who fancy only the wealthy and despise the poor are like doctors who are not concerned about healing the hands or the feet because they are at some distance from the heart. Just as this treatment would bring injury to the whole man, so in the state the weak may not be neglected without danger to the strong. The poor will rob when they are pressed through necessity; yet the judge does not think it important to pay attention to the cause, a small matter to him. These poor envy the rich, and are angered and resentful that the wealthy have so much money to lavish on jesters, dogs, harlots, asses, packhorses, and elephants. In the meantime, the poor themselves do not have the means to feed their starving children. The former proudfully and insolently flaunt their wealth, which has been wrung from these destitute and others like them.

One would hardly believe how many civil insurrections such voices of the poor have incited throughout the nations, wars in which the mobs—wrathful and burning with hate—take out their vengeance first of all upon the wealthy. The Gracchi suggest no other reason, nor did Lucius Catiline, for the anarchy which the mobs aroused; nor is it much less with the riots in our own times and regions. It will not be inappropriate to insert here a passage from Isocrates' speech, *The Areopagiticus,* which refers to the customs of the Athenians. He states:

Similarly, they acted in their relations to each other. For there was not only consensus in public matters; but in private affairs they showed the consideration of one another as is appropriate for men of common sense, members of the same homeland. Far from poor citizens envying the richer, they were as concerned about the homes of the wealthy as they were about their own, judging the prosperity of the rich as an advantage to themselves.

The affluent did not despise the poor, but considered it a reflection upon themselves that there should be poverty in the city. They underwrote the necessities of the poor, leasing plots of land to some at a moderate rental, sending others out as their business agents or negotiators, advancing to others the capital for business opportunities. They did not fear losing their investments in these measures, or worry about being despoiled of them in whole or in part. On the contrary, they felt as confident about their money as if it had been under guard at home.

A mutual danger imperils the commonwealth from the contagion of disease. It happens too often that one man has brought into the community some serious and dreadful disease, such as the plague, or syphilis, or the like, causing others to perish. What sort of situation is this, when in every church—especially at the solemn and most heavily attended feasts—one is obliged to enter into the church proper between two rows or squadrons of the sick, the vomiting, the ulcerous, the diseased with ills whose very names cannot be mentioned. And more, this is the only entrance for boys and girls, the aged and the pregnant! Do you think these are made of such iron that, fasting as they are, they are not revolted by this spectacle—especially since ulcers of this sort are not only forced upon the eyes but upon the nose as well, the mouth, and almost on the hands and body as they pass through? How shameless such begging! I will not even discuss the fact that some who have just left the side of one dead of the plague mingle with the crowd.

These two matters—how diseases may be cured and how their contagion to others can be suppressed—must not be neglected by administrators of the state. Further, a wise government, solicitous for the common good, will not leave so large a part of the citizenry in a condition of uselessness, harmful to themselves and to others. When the general funds have been expended, those without means of subsistence are driven to robbery in the city and on the highways; others commit theft stealthily; women of eligible years put modesty aside and, no longer holding to chastity, put it on sale for a bagatelle (and then, can never be persuaded to abandon this detestable practice); old women take up regular pandering and then sorcery, which promotes procuring. Children of the needy receive a deplorable upbringing. Together with their brood, the poor are cast out of the churches and wander over the land; they do not receive the sacraments and they hear no sermons. We do not know by what law they live, nor what their practices or beliefs. Actually, the discipline of the church has collapsed so completely that no ministrations are offered without an attendant charge. Clerics scorn the reference to selling, yet they force the people into recompense. Even the bishop of a diocese does not consider such shorn sheep as belonging to his fold and pasture.

So, there is no one to see that these beggars go to confession or receive communion with others at the Lord's Supper. Since they never hear instructions, they inevitably judge things by false standards and lead most disorderly lives. If it happens in some way that they come into money, they are intolerable because of their base and discreditable upbringing. So it follows that those vices (which I cited earlier) are not so much the fault of the poor as of the administrators who do not provide adequate regulations for the good government of the people. Rather, they consider themselves chosen to preside exclusively over legal suits concerning money or to pass sentences on crimes.

On the contrary, it is much more important for magistrates to work on ways of producing good citizens than on punishing or restraining evil-doers. How much less need there would be of punishment if these matters were attended to in the first place! The Romans of ancient times provided in such manner for their citizens that no one needed to beg; hence begging was forbidden in the Twelve Tables. The Athenians took the same preventive measures for their populace. Again, the Lord gave to the Jewish people a peculiar law, hard and intractable, such as became a people of similar temperament; yet in Deuteronomy He commands them to such precautions that, so far as it was within their power, there was to be no indigent or beggar among them, especially in that year of rest so acceptable to the Lord. In such manner are all people to live; for them the Lord Jesus was buried—with the Old Law and ceremonials and the "old man"—and rose again in a regeneration of life and spirit. Unquestionably, it is a scandal and disgrace that we Christians confront everywhere in our cities so many poor and indigent, we to whom no injunction has been more explicitly commanded than charity (I might say, the only one).

Wherever you turn, you encounter poverty and want, always along with those who are obliged to hold out their hands for a dole. In a state, anything ravaged or ruined by time or fortune is renewed, such as walls, ditches, ramparts, streams, institutions, customs, laws themselves; so it would be equally reasonable to reform that method of poor relief which in various ways in the passage of time has become outmoded. The most eminent men, and others interested in the welfare of the city, have devised some salutary measures: taxes have been eased; public lands have been turned over to the poor for cultivation; certain surplus funds have been distributed by the state—things which we have seen even in our own day. However, measures of this sort require specific conditions which appear only too rarely in our times. Recourse must be made, therefore, to other more appropriate and more enduring solutions.

II

IDENTIFICATION AND REGISTRATION OF THE POOR

Someone may ask me: "How do you propose to relieve such numbers?" If true charity dwelt in us, if it were truly a law (though compulsion is not necessary for one who loves), it would hold all things in common. One man would regard another's distress as though it were his own. As it is, however, no one extends his concern beyond his own home, and sometimes not even beyond his own room or himself personally. Too many are not sufficiently concerned about their own parents or children or brothers or wife. Therefore, since human countermeasures must be employed—especially among those for whom divine commands are ineffective—I suggest the following plan.

Some of the poor live in places usually called "hospitals"—the Greek word is Ptochotrophia, but I will use the more familiar word—and others beg in public; still others endure their afflictions as best they can in their own places. I define a hospital as any place where the sick are fed and nursed, where a given number of indigent persons are supported, boys and girls educated, abandoned infants nourished, the insane confined, and the blind allowed to spend their days. Rulers of states must understand that these institutions are part of their responsibilities.

No one may circumvent the founders' stipulations in setting up these institutions; these must remain inviolable. With these one should interpret not merely the words but attend primarily to their jurisdiction (as in deeds of trust) and intent (as in wills). On this point, no doubt it was the donors' desire that the funds left by them should be distributed to the best possible purposes and used in the worthiest places; they were not so much concerned by whom this should be done, or how, as that it should be done.

In the next place, there is nothing so free in the state that it could not be subject to inquiry by those who administer the government. Liberty is found in yielding obedience to the magistrates of the community rather than in that encouragement to violence or in the opportunity for widespread license in whatever direction caprice may lead. No one can remove his property from the custody and control of the state unless he gives up his citizenship. Even more, he may not even give up his life, which is of more importance and value than property. Indeed, everyone has acquired his property with the help of the state, as if it were a gift, and can keep and hold his wealth only through the state.

Therefore, going in two's and with a secretary, the Senators should visit each of these institutions and inspect it. They should write a full account of its condition, of the number of inmates, their names, who supports them there, and the reason for each person's being there. These results should be reported to the Councilors and the Senate in assembly.

Those who suffer poverty at home should be registered also, along with their family, by two Senators for each parish, their needs ascertained, their manner of living up until then, and the reason for their decline into poverty. It will be easy to discover from their neighbors what kind of individuals they are, how they live, and what their habits are. However, the testimony of one pauper should not be taken too seriously concerning another pauper, for the one would not be free from jealousy of the other. The Councilors and Senate should be informed of all these things. If someone suddenly becomes destitute, he should notify them through one of the Senators; then his situation can be judged adequately, on the basis of his condition and circumstances.

Beggars in good health who wander about with no fixed dwelling-place should submit their names, and state the reason for their mendicancy to the Senate—however, in some open place or vacant lot, so that their filth may not pollute the Senate chamber. Beggars who are ill should do likewise in the presence of two or four Senators apart, along with a doctor, so that the eyes of the entire Senate may be spared. Witnesses should be sought out by both classes of paupers to testify in regard to their manner of life.

The Senators appointed to make these examinations and perform these duties should be given authority to coerce and compel obedience, even to the point of imprisonment, so that the Senate will be aware of the recalcitrant.

III

MEANS OF PROVIDING NECESSITIES FOR THESE DISADVANTAGED

From the outset this principle must be accepted which the Lord imposed on the human race as a punishment for its many sins—that each man should eat the bread which is the fruit of his labor. When I use the word "eat" or "nourish" or "support," I do not intend to suggest food alone, but clothes, shelter, fuel, and light; in a word, everything that is related to the sustenance of the body.

None among the poor should be idle, provided, of course, that he is fit for work by his age and health. As the Apostle writes to the Thessalonians—

For even when we were with you, we commanded that if anyone will not work, then let him not eat. For we hear that some who walk among you in disorderly manner do not work at all, but are mere busybodies. Now, those who are like that we denounce, and exhort in the Lord Jesus Christ that they work in silence and eat their own bread.

And the Psalmist promises a double joy, both in this life and in the next, to him who has eaten out of the labor of his own hands. Therefore, no one must be permitted to live indolently in the state; rather, as in a well-ordered home, everyone has his own role and its related tasks to perform. As the saying goes, "By doing nothing, men learn to do evil."

Breakdowns in health and age must be taken into consideration. However, in order that a pretense of sickness or infirmity may not be foisted on you—which happens quite frequently—the opinion of physicians must be consulted. Impostors are to be penalized. Of the able-bodied vagrants, those who are aliens should be returned to their own country—as is provided for, according to Imperial law—but they should be supplied with money for the journey. It would be inhuman to send a destitute man on a journey with no provision for the trip; otherwise such a person might question, What is this measure other than commanding him to pillage on the way? If they are from areas ravaged by war, then the teaching of Paul must be borne in mind: that among those who have been baptized in the blood of Christ, there is neither Greek nor pagan, neither Frenchman nor Lowlander, but a new and elevated creature. Hence, these should be treated as though they were native-born.

Should the native-born poor be asked whether they have learned a trade? Yes, and those who have not—if they are of suitable age—should be taught the one to which they are most strongly attracted, provided that it is practical, or else a similar or related occupation. For example, if it is not possible for him to sew clothing, he could sew what they call *caligas* (soldiers' boots). If a craft is too difficult, or if he is too slow in learning, another and easier task should be assigned to him, all the way down to one in which he could be sufficiently instructed in a very short time, such as digging, drawing water, carrying loads, pushing a wheelbarrow, serving magistrates, running errands, carrying letters or mail packets, or driving the scheduled horses.

Even those who have dissipated their fortunes in dissolute living—through gaming, harlots, excessive luxury, gluttony, and gambling—should be given food, for no one should die of hunger. However, smaller rations and more irksome tasks should be assigned to them so that they may be an example to others. Perhaps they would come to repent of their prior life and not relapse as easily into the same vices, restrained as they are by the lack of food and the duress of their tasks. They must not die of hunger, but they must feel its pangs.

Many workshops could provide them employment. The woolweavers of Armentium—indeed, craftsmen in almost all the shops—complain of the scarcity of workmen. The silkweavers of Bruges would be glad to hire almost anybody for turning the little wheels of their looms; they would pay a fairly good wage each day, including board, to such workers. Even so, they cannot find boys as apprentices because their parents say that the children bring home more from begging.

Public authority should authorize a certain number of laborers who cannot find work by themselves to be assigned to one director of a workshop. When such a worker has progressed far enough in his craft, he should open his own workshop. To these, as well as to those to whom the magistrates had assigned apprentices, contracts should be given for manufacturing the numerous items which the state uses for public purposes, such as portraits, statues, robes, sewers, ditches, buildings, and supplies required by the hospitals.

Since funds for such measures of support were originally given for the poor, they should be spent on the poor. I would like to remind bishops, theologians, and abbots of this, but will write for them elsewhere. I would hope that they would do these things spontaneously, without being urged on by me.

As for those not yet assigned to a specific work or master-artisan, they should be maintained in some place by alms for the time being; but they should not remain idle in the meantime or learn slothfulness through inactivity. In places of this sort, breakfast or dinner should be given to healthy vagrants along with enough money for travel to take them to the next city which lies on their way.

The able-bodied who remain in the hospitals like drones, living by the sweat of others, should leave and be put to work. However, some must be allowed to remain because of a given estate—such as the law of gentility—or the prerogative willed by a generous benefactor or because of having made over their property to the institution. Even in these cases, they should be obliged to work in the hospital so that the result of their labors may be shared by all. If anyone healthy and robust ask to be allowed to remain because of his love for the home and for his companions, he could be granted this favor, but on the same condition.

No one should be attracted by the money that was contributed earlier for pious works. This warning is not without foundation. For there are those who, from servants, have become masters. Ladies living delicately in splendor and luxury were originally admitted to perform works of piety; but now, having thrust out the poor or else keeping them grudgingly, they have become haughty mistresses. This office of ministration must be taken from them so that they will not grow fat from the pennies of the starving poor; so let them perform the duty which they came there to do. They should be intent upon ministering to the sick, like those widows of the early church who were so highly praised by the Apostles. In the balance of their time, they could pray, read, spin, weave, or occupy themselves in some good and honest labor—all of which Jerome advises for even the richest and most aristocratic matrons.

The blind should not be allowed to sit idle or wander about aimlessly. There are many occupations in which they might be employed. Some are suited for academic training; these should be allowed to study since their aptitude for letters is no small thing. Others are suited to the art of music; they could sing, pluck the lute, or play the flute. Others might turn weavers' wheels, work treadmills, tread winepresses, or blow bellows in the smithies. Still other blind are particularly skilled in making little boxes and chests, fruit-baskets and cages. Women who are blind could spin and wind yarn. Since it is easy enough to find employment for them, none of the blind should be willing to sit idle or avoid work. Laziness and a love of ease are the reasons for pretending they cannot do things, not physical defect.

The infirm and the aged, too, should have lighter tasks assigned them suited to their age and strength. No one is so feeble or lacking in strength that he can do nothing. It follows that the evil thoughts and affections likely in the minds of the idle will be controlled by those who are employed and intent upon work.

Then, when all the leeches have been eliminated from the hospitals, the resources of each institution should be examined, taking into account its regular expenses, annual revenues, and the money on hand. Treasure rooms and superfluous trappings should be eliminated, since they are only toys for children or misers, useless in a life of piety. Then, assign to each of the hospitals as many of the sick poor as it will seem proper, taking care that the food is not so scanty that their hunger will not be easily satisfied. This is one of the essentials in the care of those who are sick in body or mind, for invalids often grow worse from an inadequate diet. On the other hand, there should be no luxury by which they might easily fall into bad practices.

Now let us refer to the insane. Since there is nothing in the world more excellent than man, and nothing more excellent in man than his mind, particular care should be given to its welfare. It should be considered the highest of ministries to restore the mind of others to sanity, or to keep them sane and rational. Therefore, when a man of disturbed mental faculties is brought to the hospital, first of all, it must be determined whether his insanity is congenital or has resulted from some environmental cause, and whether there is hope for health or whether the case is completely hopeless. One ought to feel a compassion before such a great disaster to this noblest of human faculties. He who has suffered so should be treated with such care and delicacy that the cure will not enlarge or increase the condition, such as would result from mocking, exciting, or irritating him, approving and applauding the foolish things which he says or does, and inciting him to act more ridiculously, applying a stimulus, as it were, to his absurdity and stupidity. What could be more inhuman than to drive a man to insanity just for the sake of laughing at him and entertaining oneself with such a misfortune!

Remedies suited to the individual patient should be prescribed. Some need care and attention to their mode of living. Others need mild and gentle treatment so that, like wild animals, they may gradually grow less violent. Some require education. Some may need force and chains, but these should be used in such a way that the patients will not become the more violent because of them. Above all, as far as it is possible, tranquillity must be introduced into their minds, for it is through this that reason and mental health return.

If the hospitals cannot accommodate all the diseased beggars, one or more homes should be built, as many as are necessary, where they can be treated separately. A doctor, a pharmacist, and male and female nurses should be hired. Doing this is what nature (as well as a builder of ships) does, locating the repugnant in one place so that it may not offend the rest of the body. Likewise, those afflicted with a loathsome or contagious disease should sleep and eat their food in a place apart so that their repulsive condition, or the infection itself, may not creep over the rest of the population—or else there will never be an end to disease.

When a patient recovers, he should be treated in the same manner as the rest who are healthy. He should be sent out to work unless, out of compassion, he would prefer to remain serving in the hospital with his particular skills.

For the poor who live at home, work should be furnished by the public officials, by the hospitals, or by private citizens. If their work is not enough to supply their needs, whatever seems adequate should be added to their earnings.

Investigators into the needs of the poor should perform their task humanely and kindly. While nothing should be given if the judgment on their needs is unfavorable, still intimidation should never be applied unless deemed necessary in dealing with the refractory or the rebels against public authority.

This one law should be inviolable: "If anyone request money or exert influence in favor of a person supposedly in need, he should not receive it; instead, there should be a penalty according as the Senate sees fit." It should always be permissible to inform the Senate of the needs of others. The administrators of charities—or whoever may be appointed by the Senate—should find the balance, and give alms in proportion to the need. This is to guard against the situation in the future when wealthy men, preserving their own moneys, might demand that money which belongs to the destitute should be expended on their own servants, domestics, relatives, and friends. Such favoritism steals from those who need it so much more, as we have already seen happen in the hospitals.

IV

PROVISIONS FOR CHILDREN

A hospital must be established for abandoned children where they may be reared. If mothers are known, they should nurture the infants until the sixth year. After this age, all such children would enter a publicly supported school where they would be educated in letters and morals, and be maintained.

As far as possible, this school should be in charge of men who are trustworthy and who have a solid and broad education themselves, so that they may pour out their culture into this basic school with their own example. No greater danger for the sons of the poor exists than a cheap, inferior, and demoralizing education. In order to secure teachers of this upright character, magistrates should spare no expense. At relatively small cost, the latter will thus perform a great service to the state over which they preside.

The students should learn to live frugally, but neatly and clean, and to be content with little. They should be protected from all forms of dissipation. They must not develop habits of intemperance and gluttony, becoming slaves of the belly. Otherwise, when they are deprived of something that their appetite calls for, they will shamelessly take up begging, as we have seen some do the moment they do not get, not just the food, but even their condiments such as mustard, sauce, or some such trifle.

They should be taught not only reading and writing but, above all, the duty of a Christian and right attitudes toward things.

I suggest a similar school for girls, in which they can be taught the fundamentals of literacy. If one girl is particularly qualified for studies and is inclined to them, she should be permitted to progress farther, provided that the courses coincide with the development of her character. In addition to spinning, sewing, weaving, embroidery, cooking, and home management, all girls should be taught a virtuous perspective and morality as well as modesty, frugality, gentleness, good manners, and, primarily, chastity (convinced, as they ought to be, of the excellence of this virtue in women).

Any of the boys who are particularly skilled at letters should be retained by the school to become teachers themselves; later on, they might become candidates for the priesthood. The others should learn the trades in which they are most interested.

V

SUPERVISORS AND THEIR DUTIES

Two supervisors should be appointed every year from among the members of the Senate, eminent individuals of obvious integrity, to become acquainted with the way of life of the poor, of boys, youths, and old men alike. With regard to boys, inquiry should be made concerning their occupations, the progress they are making, the sort of lives they lead, the talents they possess, the promise they show, and, if any one of them is in trouble, who is to blame. From these, corrections can be made.

In regard to young adults and old men, the supervisors should inquire if they are living according to the laws governing them. Such investigators should also inquire most carefully concerning old women, who are master-hands at pandering and sorcery. Further, they should study whether all of these persons lead a frugal and sober life. Those who frequent gaming places and wine and beer taverns should be penalized. If reprimands have no effect, such persons should be punished severely.

A system of penalties should be devised in each state, as judged applicable by its wisest and most prestigious citizens. The same measures do not apply equally to all places and times; some men are influenced by some things, and others, by other things. In any case, the fraud of idle, lazy men must be guarded against so that deception has no profit.

I would also suggest that the supervisors investigate as well the youth who are the sons of the wealthy. It could be very valuable to the well-being of the state if they were to oblige such young men to render an account to the magistrates (as though to fathers) concerning their use of time, and what activities and occupations they follow. This could prove a greater alms than that which is distributed to the poor.

In ancient times, this service was provided by the office of Questor, or Censor, among the Romans, and among the Athenians in the court of Areopagus. When the old practices had deteriorated, they were revived by the Emperor Justinian in codifying the duties of the Questor. These included the injunction to survey all persons—both ecclesiastical and secular, of whatever rank and fortune—asking who they were, from whence they came, and for what reason they were there. That same law allowed no one to live in idleness.

VI

THE FUNDING OF THESE PROPOSALS

The above plan sounds wonderful, someone will say, but where are we to get the funds for all these projects? As I see it, not only will funds not be lacking but—I believe with complete assurance—they will abound. They will be available not only for the basic necessities of life but for extraordinary needs as well, of the sort that inevitably occur to people everywhere.

In another era when the life of Christ was still vital, all believers cast their wealth at the feet of the Apostles to be distributed by them to everyone according to need. In time, the Apostles relinquished this responsibility as not becoming for them. In truth, it was more appropriate for them to teach the community and to preach the Gospel than to spend their time in soliciting and distributing money; therefore, this duty was given to deacons. These latter did not retain it very long, for so great was their zeal for teaching and spreading Christian living that they hurried on through a blessed death to everlasting bliss. Consequently, lay persons supplied the needs of the poor. The number of Christians increased, many persons of questionable probity were admitted, and the administration of moneys began to be managed dishonestly by some of them. Out of love for the poor, bishops and priests once again assumed the responsibility for the funds collected for charity. At that time, there was nothing that men would not entrust to bishops, who were persons of tried and universally recognized integrity and fidelity, a fact mentioned by John Chrysostom.

However, as the ardor for the blood of Christ increasingly abated and the Spirit of the Lord was communicated to fewer, the Church began to copy the world and to rival it in pomp, pride, and luxury. Jerome complained that the governors of the provinces dined more sumptuously in the monastery than in the palace. This extravagance required large sums of money, and so the bishops and priests diverted to this purpose money that belonged to the poor. If only the Spirit of God would touch them and recall to their minds whence they had received it, who had given it, and for what reason! If only they would remember that out of the substance of the poor they had become powerful!

It is the obligation of bishops not only to teach, console, and correct in concerns of the souls of men but also to heal their bodies, succoring the poor from their own substance (even if that is extremely small). They would do this to their great advantage and their peace of mind if their faith in Christ were as great as they wish the faith of others to be. Of course, this is a common failing: all of us mercilessly demand in another the virtue which we do not ourselves possess.

In a word, bishops should follow the example of Paul, to be absolutely perfect in charity that they might be all things to all men, neither deferring to the mighty nor despising the lowly, but placing themselves on the same level with all men in order to help them and edify them, according to the word of Christ. Bishops, abbots, and other officials of the Church (if only they wished it) could relieve a very large portion of the existing poverty out of their large incomes; if they do not do so, Christ will avenge it!

Turmoil and civil disorder must always be avoided because this is a greater evil than the misappropriation of the funds for the poor. However vast wealth may be, it should never be so highly revered that men would take up arms on its account. Above all, respect must be had for the general peace, as Christ taught, and also Paul, restating his master. Nor should the poor yearn for any disorder in the state whereby they would profit. Rather, it is proper for them to be unconcerned about the times, devoting themselves day and night to meditation upon the end of this life's journey to that haven and fatherland where they will hear, 'Lazarus once suffered in his lifetime; now, therefore, he will be comforted and refreshed."

The annual revenue of hospitals should be calculated as a whole. I have no doubt that, when work has been assigned to those able to do it, not only will the income be sufficient to care for those who live there; it will be enough to care for those who live on the outside as well. I am told that the wealth of hospitals in any town you can name is so great that, if it were properly administered, there would be more than enough for supplying all the ordinary as well as unforeseen and extraordinary needs of the citizens.

Wealthy institutions should share their superfluous income with the poorer; and if the poorer are not desperate, the surplus should go to those suffering in secret. Let Christian charity diffuse itself thus not only throughout the whole state—making, as it were, one harmonious household, with common interests among them all, each a friend to all—but spread out and enclose the whole Christian world. Let it come to pass, as we read it was among the Apostles:

The multitude of those who believed were of one heart and one soul. No one of them said that anything he possessed was his own. Rather, they held all things in common . . . neither was there among them any who lacked for anything.

So it follows that wealthy hospitals and rich men will send their contributions to neighboring places when there are none in their own city who need help, or even to distant places where there are greater needs. This is true Christian action.

For each hospital the Senate should appoint by vote two overseers, who are respected, God-fearing men. They should render a yearly account of their administration. If their performance is satisfactory, they could continue in office; if not, new officers should be selected.

Many a man at his death wills something to the poor, according to his means. He should be encouraged to stipulate that money for the poor be deducted from the pomp of his funeral. If this were so, such a funeral would be more acceptable to God and would still not lack honor among men. Those about to depart this life should have no concern for praise and glory except from God. At the funeral, meat would then be distributed, and bread, as well as money or supplies. This should be at the discretion of those who have charge of the decedent's estate, both on the occasion of the funeral and on the anniversary of his death.

In the next place, if money is willed for the poor, the overseers should investigate in what manner it is dispensed, so that it may not be given to those not in need of it.

If all these sources of money are not sufficient, then little boxes should be placed in three or four of the principal churches of the town where attendance is largest. Into these boxes everyone would be able to deposit as much as his devotion would suggest. There would not be a devout person who would not prefer to place a large sum therein than give a small sum directly into the hands of wandering beggars. The boxes would not be set out every week but only when need demanded it. Two honest and trustworthy men would be in charge of them, men chosen by the Senate not so much for wealth as for a mind free from greed and selfishness, a qualification of highest importance for such a position.

The policy should be to collect not as much as possible but, generally, only enough to suffice from week to week (perhaps a little more) lest the collectors become accustomed to handling large sums of money, and the same thing happen to them as to those in charge of the hospitals. What the practice in this state is, I do not know—nor do I seek to know, since I am intent on my studies. However, I have heard that in Spain the elders of a family would enrich their own houses greatly from the wealth of hospitals, feeding themselves and their families instead of the poor, keeping these homes filled with relatives, so that the hospitals actually have few paupers. These things are the result of easy access to so much ready money.

In a similar vein, no lands for farming (which would offset the difficulties of the poor) should be purchased. This furnishes a pretext to the directors of the hospitals to retain the money given them while the full sum is being collected for the investment and being kept until it is proper to buy. In the meantime, the pauper wastes away from hunger and want, and dies.

If there is a large sum of money in the hands of those who have charge of public finances, it should be circulated, as I said before, and sent to needier localities. For a large sum of money magnifies the desire for it to such a degree that those who handle it are more reluctant to withdraw something from it than they would be from a small amount. Whatever is strictly necessary should be kept in the hands of the Senate under oath and protected by bans and threats, so that it will not be diverted to any other use. It should be expended at the first opportunity so that it will not become customary to keep any of it undisclosed. There will never be a lack of persons who need aid, as Our Lord predicted, "The poor you have always with you."

Care should be exercised that the priests, under cover of their prayers and masses, do not turn the money to their own pockets. They are adequately cared for and need nothing more.

If it happens that voluntary contributions do not suffice, wealthy men should be approached by the overseers and asked to aid the poor whom God has committed to the latter's zealous care. At least the hospital could borrow what is needed; if the wealthy insist on it, this loan could be repaid later in good faith when alms are more plentiful.

Besides this, the state itself should deduct something from public expenses, such as from funds for solemn feasts, gifts to honored guests, state-financed entertainments for foreign ambassadors, and the largesse of money which is distributed to the people on special occasions, annual games, and processions. All these contribute only to a waste of time, to pride, and to ambition. I do not doubt that a prince would be just as well pleased, if not more so, if he were welcomed with less display, provided he knew for what good purpose the money, customarily poured out at his coming, was being spent. If he did not take to this well, he would indeed be childishly conceited and stupidly ambitious. However, if the state did not want to do this, then at least it could lend what it might later recoup at a time more promising for alms.

Almsgiving should always be voluntary, as Paul said, "Each man . . . according as he has decided in his heart, not grudgingly or from obligation." No one should be forced to do good, otherwise the very concept of *doing good* is lost. I do not doubt that by these means there will be sufficient and even more. However, in so holy a business, we should not measure ourselves solely by human strength, but place our reliance primarily on God. He will bless righteous undertakings, increasing for the rich the sources of their charity, as well as the alms of the poor who modestly ask, gratefully receive, and prudently spend. The Lord provides for all: "His is the earth and the fullness thereof." He created all things abundantly for our use, asking in return only a ready and genuine good will, and a grateful love for so many immeasurable blessings.

Many examples prove that when a holy work has been undertaken by men with some anxiety and even hopelessness on their part lest the funds for it should not be sufficient, as the work progressed it has been so blessed that even those who have charge of it are forced to wonder by what hidden ways resources have opened. You will remember one experience, typical of many, in your own school for poor boys which you established ten years ago with such minimum funds that not more than eighteen boys could be maintained there. You were concerned that you would not be able to maintain the institution. Now, more or less one hundred boys are supported there, and the funds have grown so large that even more could be assisted. When extra boys arrive, there is always something for them to eat.

Undoubtedly it is by the universal bounty of God that everything is maintained and augmented, lives and grows, not by wealth and private resources or human counsels. Hence, in pious undertakings, it would be impious to gloat over your own talents; rather, rejoice in the confidence you have in Him to Whom all things are possible.

As for the unemployed poor themselves, they should learn not to make provisions for the distant future, for this increases their sense of human security and lessens their dependence on God. They should not rely on human assistance but on Christ alone, Who has exhorted us to relinquish all concerns for our sustenance to Him and His Father Who feeds and clothes those creatures that neither sow nor reap, weave or spin. The poor should lead an angelic life, so to speak, intent on prayer first for themselves and then for the weal of those by whom they have been assisted, so that the Lord Jesus might consider them worthy to receive recompense a hundredfold in everlasting blessings.

VII

ASSISTING THOSE WHO SUFFER SUDDEN
OR SECRET MISFORTUNE

Relief should be given not only to the poor who are without day-to-day necessities of life, but also to those on whom some sudden calamity has fallen, such as captivity in war, imprisonment for debt, fire, shipwreck, floods, all kinds of sicknesses, or any of those numerous catastrophes that bring disaster to ordinary homes. To these unfortunate individuals may be added young girls whom poverty has driven to prostitution. It is intolerable in any state—I will not say Christian, nor even heathen, only provided one live in a community where men live as humans—that, where some of the citizens so give themselves to extravagances as to squander huge sums on a sepulchre, palace, useless building, banquets, or public offices, for lack of a few pennies the chastity of a virgin is tempted, the health and life of an honest man is threatened, or a husband is forced to desert his wife and children.

Captives must be ransomed, an action mentioned by the ancient philosophers (Aristotle, Cicero, and others) as one of the noblest acts of benevolence. First attention should be given to those who suffer a cruel servitude among enemies, such as the Christians who are in the power of the Turks and are daily in peril of renouncing their faith. Similar consideration should be taken for the businessmen and noncombatants who have fallen into the hands of the enemy. Armed combatants who have been captured deserve the least pity since they are the cause of the ills of others.

Of those in prisons, the first to consider are those who have fallen into poverty and bankruptcy through misfortune rather than their own fault; and then attention should be given to those who have been imprisoned for a long time. The man who has been precipitated from his once happy circumstances into misery through no fault of his own is to be greatly pitied, whether because he represents the mutual fate of humanity and stands as a symbol of the experiences of all men, or because he suffers the most acutely through a vestigial recollection of former happiness.

Men of breeding should not have to wait until they disclose their needs themselves. They should be diligently sought out and assisted secretly, such as Arcesilaus did, and many others similar, who placed a large sum of money under the pillow of a sleeping friend, a man both poor and ill, who concealed both facts from a feeling of shame. Then when the troubled individual awoke, he found relief without any injury to his honest pride. For as a principle in assisting, through public charity, a man who has been reared in gentility, care should be exercised not to wound his pride, which he may value more than the relief, however acceptable and useful that may be.

The same men to whom we assigned the supervision of the parishes should also investigate concealed needs of this sort and report them to the Senate and to men of wealth, at the same time withholding the names of the deprived and the amount of assistance needed. On the other hand, it might be better if even those poor would accept charity openly so that they can know whom to thank; further, there would be no suspicion on either side as, for instance, that those through whom it is given have funneled off some of the money. This openness would not do if the rank of the destitute man is so high that he ought not to be exposed to the embarrassment.

"But," someone will object, "if men of that class are to be assisted too, where will be the end of giving?" Indeed, what more ideal situation can be imagined than the boundlessness of charity? You have said something extremely petty—I was hoping that you would deplore the fact that at some future time there would be none left on whom to bestow compassion. Indeed, you ought to wish, for the sake of your neighbor, that there would come a time when none would need the wealth of others; for your own sake, you should hope that you would never lack the opportunity of such great profit to yourself, securing eternal blessings in exchange for things liable to varying fortunes and passing fancies.

It seems to me, in the present state of things, that these suggestions should be implemented. It may not be expedient in every city and in every circumstance to institute everything I have prescribed. Wise men in every nation will perceive this, and will consult the best interests of their own states. Still, the overall aim, intention, and goal that I have outlined will, I believe, be expedient and necessary always and in every place. If it is not possible for all these matters to be carried out at once—perhaps because traditional practices run contrary to innovation—it should be feasible with ingenuity to introduce the more moderate reforms first, and after that gradually those considered more extreme.

VIII

CONCERNING THOSE WHO WILL OPPOSE THESE PROPOSALS

Although virtue is most beautiful and desirable in itself, it nevertheless has many enemies who are exceedingly irritated by the very notion of it and its excellence, as well as by its attacks—fierce and uncompromising—upon their dissipated lives. The world, past and present, fights against the law of Christ whose brightness neither the darkness of sinners nor the vitiated eyes of evil men can withstand or endure.

So in the matter being discussed: although everything refers to the provision for the needs of man and the relief of the poverty-stricken (as anyone can easily judge, provided he is a fair, unbiased critic), still there will be no lack of persons to misinterpret and object, even though the thrust toward humaneness is made. For example, when certain individuals hear that this proposes nothing else than the elimination of the poor, they assume that paupers will be banished in person and cry out against the inhumanity of thus evicting those miserable individuals. As if we would desire to drive them out, or do anything to make them more miserable! This is not our purpose; rather, it is to free them from their distress, their struggles, and their perpetual misfortunes so that they may live more humanly and be treated with compassion.

There are some who would like to be thought of as theologians who cite a passage from the Gospel, without reference to the context in which it is located, where Christ our Lord and God prophesied, "The poor you will always have with you." What of that? Did He not predict future scandals? And Paul—that there would be heresies? Shall we therefore not assist the poor, or live unoffensively or resist heresies, for fear that we might prove the prophecies false? God forbid! Christ did not predict that the poor would always be with us because this is what He desired, or that scandals would eventuate because this is what He hoped for. In fact, He recommends nothing to us more explicitly than the relief of the poor, condemning those who cause this deplorable condition.

For He knows the weakness through which we fall into poverty, and He knows our malice through which we are reluctant to raise up a fallen man, preferring him to remain lying almost dead, and wasted. For this reason He says that we shall always have the poor with us; the same thing can be said in regard to the prophecy of sin.

Concerning heresies, Paul maintained that they would come because of the corrupted nature of man, defiled as it is with many vices. Yet he wished them to be resisted when they arose, as he said to Titus: "The bishop should exhort with sound doctrine and confound the dissidents." So in these predictions Christ does not command us to act in that manner, but sees that we will. In the same line of thinking, these proposals of mine will not eliminate poverty but will relieve it; they will not prevent a man from becoming a pauper but will preclude his remaining one for long by a prompt offer of a hand to help him to his feet.

I wish we were able to eliminate poverty completely in this city. I do not worry that Christ's words will be judged false. There would be so many remaining who would be poor in other respects. It is not only those without money who are poor but those who lack bodily vitality, physical well-being, and mental health and sanity, as was explained at the beginning of this work.

Moreover, he must be called poor, even if he has money, to whom—whether in a hospital or in his own home—delicate food is supplied which has not been obtained by his own industry and labor but through the kindness of another. Tell me, who act more humanly—those who leave the poor to rot in their filth, squalor, vice, crime, shamelessness, immodesty, ignorance, madness, misfortune, and misery?—or those who devise a way by which they may rescue them from that life and lead them into a mode of living, more social, cleaner, and wiser, clearly salvaging so many men who were formerly lost and useless? We are acting here in the same manner as the medical profession who cannot eradicate diseases completely from the population but bend every effort to cure them.

If only the law of Christ were more deeply rooted in our minds and hearts, that it might be more effective than medical knowledge! Then it might happen that there would be no paupers among us, as there were none in the early Church, according to the account of Luke in the Acts of the Apostles—nor scandals or heresies. However, our sins encumber us; men continue to profess the name of Christian not so much in their heart and by the action of their lives as by their mouths; hence, there will always be paupers and scandals and heresies.

In addition, perhaps there will be some men, as is likely in public office, who—in order to be judged wise so as to acquire influence for that reason—approve of nothing except what they have proposed. Surely these men have an erroneous concept not only of men but of God, if they believe—and wish others to be so persuaded—that God has been ineffective in all His other acts of creation, but has poured out upon these "thinkers" all the mental power of ingenuity, judgment, and wisdom. In this matter, Job said sarcastically, "Are you then the only man, and shall wisdom die with you?" I would not deny that there are some men who have such initiative, skill, and keenness of judgment that, in thinking and in deliberating, they generate more ideas than the rest of mankind. But even for that reason, to judge that which has been conceived by one's self as best is to become a man of arrogance without experience, as Terrence says of administrators "who judge nothing of value except what they do themselves."

Specifically, I anticipate two classes of men to be hostile to these plans: first, the very ones whom this philanthropy is intended to benefit; and, second, those who will be ousted from the management of funds. In the first case, some have grown so accustomed to their squalor and filth and misery that they resent being raised out of it. Captivated as they are by a certain sweetness of inertia and idleness, they think activity, labor, industry, and frugality more painful than death. How difficult, then, the task of doing good among these, since their depravity interprets kindness as injury! How odious of them to receive charity haughtily, as if offended, and to interpret it as an insult! This invidious attitude is very like that of the Jews who persecuted with death the Author of life because He showed them kindness, helped them, and brought them health, salvation, and light. They heaped insults on Him in return for the charity poured out on all who would accept it. Immersed in pride, arrogance, ambition, and avarice, they judged it an affront to be liberated from those demanding masters. In the same way, these poor, buried in squalor, filth, shame, idleness, and crime, think they are being dragged into slavery if their condition is ameliorated. We could imitate the true Christ Himself Who was not diverted from doing good by the ingratitude of those who received His advantages.

Consideration should be given not so much to what a man would like, as to what is good for him to have, not what pleases him but what is expedient for him. In time, they will recognize this value when they return to a more positive mind and will say, "The Senate of Bruges saved us against our will." But should you indulge them and follow along with their desires—if even for a moment they recover sight and reason—undoubtedly they will say, "The Senate ruined us with love." This is the complaint which every son, indulged in too freely, makes of his father. The poor so indulged will despise those by whom they have been assisted to their destruction.

In order that this may not occur, let us treat them as experienced physicians treat delirious patients—or wise fathers, their rebellious children—seeking their true good, no matter the resistance and the clamor. In a word, it is the duty of the ruler of the state not to be disturbed by what this one or that one or a given few think about the laws and administration, so long as he has consulted with the common good of the entire state. For laws are of benefit even to the law-breakers themselves by correcting and checking them in their wrongdoing.

Those who have been handling the funds for the poor will be annoyed at being removed from office. They will search out an eloquent vocabulary with which to exaggerate the enormity of the proposal: "This, these matters should be left alone.... What has been confirmed by years of approval should not be interfered with.... It is dangerous to introduce new practices.... The stipulations of founders should not be changed.... Everything is close to ruin."

To these we reply: "First, will not good practices weaken that which has been rooted in evil customs?" They will not dare to descend into that argument. Then: "Which is better?—what we are attempting to introduce, or what they wish to retain?" More: "If nothing is to be changed, why have they themselves gradually altered the first regulations established by the founders of an institution to such a degree that those in force today run counter to the original?"

Let the records be opened, let the memories of old men be questioned. It will be discovered how much the present administration differs from that when the institution was new, and while the founder was still alive or only recently deceased. Here we have caught them on a crucial matter. We do not wish to change the original organization; we will not tolerate the violation of the founder's intent, for in every will this is the first—or, rather, the only—issue. The original intent can be discovered from records and the memory of many individuals. As for the will of the founder, who does not understand that these men left their money and endowments, not that the rich might be sated but that the poor might be supported, even as they pray for their deceased benefactors that they might be forgiven their sins and be received by God into His heavenly dwelling?

Now if these objectors raise too much opposition, they will certainly make it clear to all that they are looking out for their own interests instead of that of the poor. We undertake a responsibility for the poor, and yet they oppose it—what do they have in view? If it is for their own interests, they stand convicted of avarice, and make it clear that they have managed things for their own advantage and not for the poor. Such avarice is not only ignoble but is absolutely pernicious and detestable. Since it is a crime to steal anything from a wealthy man, how much more scandalous is it to rob the poor! From the rich man, it is money which is stolen; from the poor, it is life.

If, however, it is the poor for whom they are concerned, the Senate wishes the poor to be supported even more generously. Is it any concern of these individuals by whom poor relief is provided, so long as it is done, and done as well as possible?—as by the Senate in whom confidence has been placed with good reason in the past. As St. Paul said, "That Christ may be preached—in what manner, I do not care, provided only that He is preached."

However, they wish to run the work themselves. If they have respect for God, they will joyfully concede; but if for men, their ambition has been found out. Further, would they dare to complain because you do not offer yourselves as ministers of their ambitions and avarice? Indeed, if you remain silent, are you not abetting them? I will pass over things which might be said on this matter if their long-term administration were to be examined. I will not be mired in this bog; I will not stir up this mud. But in truth, they would have no small honor—if they did not oppose these measures, and if they did not hold on to the money entrusted to them or deposited in their keeping—if they advanced the interests of the poor, devoted themselves to promoting the harmony of the state, and proved themselves such friends of the public good that they consider it their personal possession.

IX

NOTHING SHOULD STAND IN THE WAY OF
CARRYING OUT THESE PROPOSALS

The most eloquent comments have been made by classical writers on every sort of virtue, while their acts were of highest import and dignity. Yet they never conducted themselves with such constancy, courage, and worthiness as when loyalty to their country and love of their fellow citizens, implanted in their hearts, caused them to endure misrepresentations, unjust accusations, curses, and insults with undisturbed and resolute minds. They did not deviate a hair's breadth for that reason from their determination to aid their nation, even when the very ones who would be most helpful censured and condemned their actions.

Prominent among the number of such men are Miltiades, Themistocles, Scipio, and above all Epaminandos the Theban and Quintus Fabius Maximus of Rome. The latter knew that Hannibal could be defeated not by force but by delay, and therefore he prolonged the war with stalling actions, convinced that this was the only hope for victory. Many idle and craftily argumentative men complained of these tactics, saying that Fabius was doing this by agreement with Hannibal, or from ambition—that he might remain longer in power as the chief officer of the state—or from cowardice and fear, that they would abrogate his power.

As a matter of fact, Minucius, the Master of Horse, was made equal to the Dictator himself by popular vote, which had never been heard of before. The old man was undaunted by the calumny and folly of his fellow citizens and persisted in his plans, bringing his people to victory. Undoubtedly, Hannibal would have conquered the land if the strategy of Fabius had not thwarted him. The event declared how great a mind that hero possessed, what insight he had, what love for his country and his fellowmen.

These little verses about him have been universally popular, ancient and crude though they are, but eloquent and enthusiastic in their praise:

> One man with his delaying restored
>   everything to us;
> Nor did he place common opinion
>   above the common good;
> Therefore, more and more men now
>   enlarge his glory.

Others of similar mind performed noble deeds even though they did not know God (since, for them, the sun of Christianity had not arisen). They were merely acting as they had been taught, or were seeking honor and fame for their country.

How much greater and nobler should our actions be! We have witnessed the one Christ despise—indeed, disdain and score—human power. For us, that most glorious sun has dawned, and we have been reared in the true faith. To us charity has been commended and commanded, with a heavy penalty if we neglect the command and a great reward if we execute it. The reward will be amplified according to the suffering we endure for the grace of God.

Therefore, this plan must not merely be approved; it must be adopted and put into operation. It is not enough to have good intentions unless you also put your hand to the work when occasion arises. It is not appropriate that those who are urged and spurred on by divine commands should be held back by human obstacles, especially since material and spiritual benefits accrue to both the state and the individual.

X

THE MATERIAL AND SPIRITUAL ADVANTAGES
WHICH WILL RESULT FROM
THESE MEASURES

1. Tremendous honor adheres in the state in which no beggar is seen, for a great multitude of paupers argues malice and apathy in the citizenry and neglect of the public good by the magistrates.

2. Fewer thefts, acts of violence, robberies, murders, and capital offenses will be committed. Pandering and sorcery will be less frequent. This follows because the poverty will be mitigated which drives men first into vices and bad habits and then encourages and provokes crimes like the above.

3. Greater peace will prevail where everyone is provided for.

4. Greater concord will prevail. The poor will not envy the wealthy, but will esteem them as benefactors; the rich will not turn away from the destitute in suspicion, but will esteem them as the reason for their bounty and the objects of their rightful charity. Nature demands that we love those to whom we give support; thus, love begets love.

5. It will be safer, healthier, and pleasanter to attend churches and to dwell in the city. The hideousness of ulcers and diseases will no longer be imposed on the general viewing, eliminating a spectacle revolting to nature and even to the most humane and compassionate mind. Those of small means will not be forced to give alms through pressure. If a man is inclined to give, he will not be deterred either by the great multitude of beggars or by the fear of giving to someone unworthy.

6. The state will gain enormously. More citizens will become more virtuous, more law-abiding, and more useful to the nation. Everyone will hold the state dearer in which—or by means of which—they are sustained. Nor will they participate in revolution or sedition. Women will withdraw from their pernicious practices, young women from dangers to their modesty, old women from their evil designs. Boys and girls will be taught letters, religion, temperance, and self-support, all of which form the basis of an upright, honest, pious life. Finally, everyone will exercise judgment, sensitivity, and piety. They will live among men as educated and disciplined persons, observing human laws. They will hold back

their hands from violence, serving God truly and in good faith. They will be men. They will be what they are called, Christians. What else is this, I ask, than restoring many thousands of men to themselves and winning them for Christ! That is heaven's profit, for innumerable souls will be liberated through religion.

Some know that they ought to discharge the duties of charity, yet they do not perform what has been commanded; others are repelled by the unworthiness of the applicants; others withdraw because their good intention is embarrassed by the great number, and they are drawn in the opposite direction, as it were, uncertain where first or most effectively to bestow their money. They see so many oppressed by want that in a sort of despair they succor no one, feeling that whatever is given is too little, like sprinkling a drop of water here and there on raging flames of fire.

However, if our plan is adopted, those who have means will give them generously, delighted that things are so carefully and exactingly managed. In being sure that their contributions are well placed, they will help mankind, according to the commands of Christ, and win His generous favor. Undoubtedly, many wealthy men of other cities—who have not in similar fashion made the affairs of the poor their concern—will send generous contributions here, where they know funds are wisely spent and aid given to those most in need. Added to this, God will protect as His own a people who are compassionate, and make them truly blessed.

Listen to the kind of nation properly termed blessed according to the testimony, not of an ordinary man but of a prophet—

> From the peril of sword save me;
>> rescue me from the power of aliens
>> who tell nothing but lies,
>> who are prepared to swear to falsehood!
> May our sons be like plants
>> growing strong from their earliest days,
> our daughters like corner-statues,
>> carvings fit for a palace;
> may our barns overflow
>> with every possible crop;
> may the sheep in our fields be counted
>> in their thousands and tens of thousands;
> may our cattle be stout and strong;
>> and may there be an end of raids and exile,
>> and of panic in our streets.
> Happy the nation of whom this is true,
>> happy the nation whose God is Yahweh!

Nor will temporal blessings be lacking, as it was written of the widow who gave food to Elias. Also, the Psalmist sings of that nation in which the Lord dwells:

I will bless her provisions with riches,
I will satisfy her with bread.

And in another place he says, speaking to the same nation:

He has granted you peace on your frontiers,
He has fed you on the finest wheat.

Seriously, an increase of mutual love is beyond all things because it dispenses charity near and far, honestly and joyfully, without suspicion of unworthiness. Hereafter, we shall obtain that celestial reward which we have shown is prepared for the man of charity.

REFERENCES

1. Modern historians utilize sociology extensively in their conceptualizing. A classic statement in this mode is Alfred Von Martin's *Sociology of the Renaissance* (New York: Harper & Row, 1963 [from the German, 1932]).

2. Lynn Thorndike, *A History of Magic and Experimental Science*, 8 vols. (New York: Macmillan Co., 1929-58), vols. 5 and 6, *Sixteenth Century*.

3. *The City of God*, trans. "J.H." [John Healey] (London, 1620), STC 916, book 8, chap. 35, p. 280. Reference is made to geomancy, pyromancy, capnomancy, augury, coscinomancy, axinomancy, botanomancy, necromancy, astrology, cleromancy, chiromancy, physiognomy, ichthyomancy, and hydromancy, in addition to techniques of interpreting dreams, visions, thunder, lightning, noises, sneezings, and voices.

4. Foster Watson, *Vives: On Education* (Cambridge, England: Cambridge University, 1913), pp. 231-33.

5. Sidney Lens, *Poverty: America's Enduring Paradox* (New York: Thomas Crowell Co., 1969), pp. 2 ff.

6. Henry de Vocht, ed., *Literae Virorum Eruditorum Ad Franciscum Craneveldium* (Louvain: Libraire Universitaire, 1929), Letter 72, n.1. The cup was probably made by Peter Dominicle, goldsmith of Bruges. See also Ep. 95, intro.: Goclenius translated Lucian's *Hermotimus*, dedicated to Thomas More, October 29, 1522, for which he received a cup of gold coins.

7. F. R. Salter, *Some Early Tracts on Poor Relief* (Preface by Sidney Webb) (London: Methuen & Co., 1926), p. xx. This collection includes the tracts by Luther and Zwingli, as well as the legislation of Ypres (1529), Rouen (1535), and England (1531 and 1536).

8. E. M. W. Tillyard, *The Elizabethan World Picture* (New York: Macmillan Co., 1942), chap. 4, "The Chain of Being."

9. Fritz Caspari, *Humanism and the Social Order in England* (Chicago: University of Chicago Press, 1954), pp. 6-7, 118.

10. One man who judges Vives to be more the empiricist than he probably was, yet enlarges on some valuable insights into Vives's reality-oriented theorizing, is Hiram Haydn, *The Counter-Renaissance* (New York: Scribners, 1950), pp. 17-18, 19, 21, 84, 86, 98-104, 251 ff. Vives differed from his contemporaries in spanning the chasm between the theoretical and the practical, between intellectual proposals and actual reforms. See E. Harris Harbison, "The Intellectual as a Social Reformer: Machievelli and Thomas More," *Rice Institute Pamphlets* 44, No. 3 (October 1957): 1-47. The latter humanist is characterized by an enthusiasm for the classics and for Christ without experiencing a personal responsibility for carrying implicit consequences to conclusions.

11. Salter, *Some Early Tracts*, introductory notes to each original source.

12. Edward Viles and F. J. Furnival, eds., *Fraternitye of Vacabondes (and Others)* (Early English Text Society; London: N. Trubner, 1869); J. Meadows Cowper, ed., *Henry Brinkler's Complaynt of Roderyck Mors* (Early English Text Society; London: N. Trubner, 1874); F. J. Furnival, ed., *Four Supplications* (Early English Text Society; London: N. Trubner, 1871).

13. "H. A." [Henry Arthington], *Provision for the Poore* (London, 1597), STC 798.

14. *A Politic Plot. . .*, London, 1580, STC 13531.

15. E. M. Leonard, *The Early History of English Poor Relief* (new impression; New York: Barnes and Noble, 1965), pp. 1-10. The classic statement remains unchallenged: William Ashley, *An Introduction to English Economic History and Theory* (new impression; New York: Augustus M. Kelly, 1966), Book 2, chap. 5, "The Relief of the Poor," pp. 305-76.

16. Gregorio Majansius, ed., *Joannis Lodovicus Vivis Valentini, Opera Omni*, 8 vols.; Valencia, 1783 (Greg reprint), vol. 4, pp. 421-64.

17. See Wilbur K. Jordan's three studies, *Philanthropy in England, 1480-1600; The Charities of London, 1480-1660; The Charities of Rural England, 1480-1660* (London: Allen & Unwin, 1959, 1960, 1961).

18. Carl E. Steinbicker, *Poor Relief in the Sixteenth Century* (Washington, D.C.: Catholic University of America, 1937), pp. 105-9, in which reference is made to Walter John Marx, *The Development of Charity in Medieval Louvain*, pp. 37 ff.

19. Leonard, *Early History*, p. 17. Nonpolemical research is showing that monasteries, as in England, were not so seriously remiss in charity as they were unorganized for uniform poor relief from one locality to another. See David Knowles, *Religious Orders in England* (3 vols.; Cambridge, England: Cambridge University Press, 1959), vol. 3, pp. 264-66; and Ashley, *An Introduction*, pp. 313-14.

20. Sidney and Beatrice Webb, *English Poor-Law History* ("English Local Government"

series, vol. 7 [London: Archon Books, 1927; new impression, 1963]), p. 404.
21.   Webb, *English Poor-Law History*, p. 408. See also R. H. Tawney, *Religion and the Rise of Capitalism* (London: J. Murray, 1929), p. 253.
22.   Knowles, *Religious Orders*, vol. 3, p. 264.
23.   Webb, *English Poor-Law History*, pp. 402-3. Steinbicker (*Poor Relief in the Sixteenth Century*, p. 109) indicates that poor relief as structured through the Council of Trent rejected the pooling of relief revenues into a common chest, civil supervision, prohibition of begging, localization and centralization of relief agencies, and regulation of the needy themselves. In a word, the post-Renaissance, post-Reformation Church opted for measures contrary to Vives's general concepts, which were suspect because of being "pro-Lutheran."
24.   The details on Bruges are primarily from Malcolm Letts, *Bruges and Its Past* (London: A. G. Berry, 1924), pp. 54-58. See also Salter, *Some Early Tracts*, pp. xi, xv, 3, 4, 6, 23-25, 35.
25.   Lodovico Guichardini, *A Description of the Low Countreys*, trans. T. Danett (London, 1593), STC 12463, p. 93. This delightful travelogue, completed no more than twenty years after Vives's lifetime, must be considered descriptive of the Bruges that Vives knew.
26.   Steinbicker, *Poor Relief in the Sixteenth Century*, p. 112.
27.   Bruges was not so cold-hearted as to neglect its poor in the interim. The usual means of assistance, a liberal policy toward prisoners in the Steen, and schools and homes for orphans were continued. An institution for the insane, dating from the fourteenth century, was maintained. See Letts, *Bruges and Its Past*, p. 111.
28.   Steinbicker, *Poor Relief in the Sixteenth Century*, pp. 195-222. This otherwise valuable survey is spotted with polemic and opinion diluting its scholarship.
29.   Much of this section of the narrative is summarized from my introductory essay in *J. L. Vives' Introduction to Wisdom* (New York: Teachers College Press, 1968), pp. 1-36. See also de Vocht, *Literae Virorum Eruditorum*, Ep. 136, 11. 38-39.
30.   Josse Lauwereyns (? - Nov. 6, 1527), had risen to diplomatic prominence as a skilled debater. In 1522 he was appointed president of the Grand Council of Mechlin, and he played a leading role in political matters of the time. Vives and others admired him for his "erudition, experience, and eloquence," but he committed the serious error of not supporting Erasmus against the Carmelite, Baechem, in the religio-political office of inquisitor for the Netherlands. From then on, his reputation as a student of languages and literature deteriorated among the humanists. See de Vocht, *Literae Virorum Eruditorum*, Eps. 74, 99, 123, and 156, with their introductions; P. S. Allen, *Erasmi Epistolae* (12 vols.; Oxford: Oxford University Press, 1913-47), Eps. 1299, 1303.
31.   Salter, *Some Early Tracts*. Ashley (*An Introduction*, p. 374) states that Vives's influence has been treated well and for the first time by Ehrle *(Beitrage sur Geschichte . . . der Armenpflege)*, although without sufficient reference to the contemporary religious thought among Protestant theologians or to other cities than Ypres.
32.   Louis de Praet (1488-1555) had been a student of the Brethren of the Common Life, had studied at Louvain, and had remained a steadfast devotee of things literary in spite of his numerous political offices. Charles V would recall him on occasion for personal consultations, so highly did the Emperor value his advice. In addition to *On Assistance to the Poor*, Vives also dedicated to him *De Consultatione*, written while at Oxford in 1523. In 1529 the Spaniard was still referring to him as "one of the glories of Ghent." See de Vocht, *Literae Virorum Eruditorum*, introductions to Eps. 39, 55, 150; also Allen, *Erasmi Epistolae*, Ep. 1847.
33.   Commentaries on the *Utopia* are too numerous to cite separately. H. H. Hexter, in *More's Utopia: The Biography of an Idea* (Priceton, N.J.: Princeton University Press, 1952), has a number of relevant comments (see pp. 73, 77, 78, 144-46); others suggest that all related bibliography on More has been classified and cited in Frank and Majie Sullivan, *Moreana* (4 vols; Los Angeles, Calif.: Loyola University, 1964-68).
34.   de Vocht, *Literae Virorum Eruditorum*, Ep. 157, 1. 45.
35.   Ibid., Ep. 163, 11. 1-20.
36.   Ibid., Ep. 167, 11. 1-6.
37.   Ibid., Ep. 171, 11.
38.   Ibid., Ep. 185, 11. 12-15.
39.   Ibid., Ep. 193, 3-18. Much of the letter is taken up by an enumeration of the misprints of the edition by de Crooc.
40.   Salter, *Some Early Tracts*, pp. 33 ff.
41.   de Vocht, *Literae Virorum Eruditorum*, Ep. 248, 11. 1-6.
42.   Ibid., Ep. 61, 1. 4. According to the colophon of *De Subventione*, he had finished it "XVI, Calendas, Aprileis A. MDXXV." Between 1519 and 1523 he had been dean of the Bruges guild of booksellers. He apparently built up a lively trade in religious engravings of his own making, and did not print extensively.
43.   Thomas Marshall, trans., *The Forme and Maner of Subventione or Helping for Por*

People (London: Thomas Godfrey, 1535), STC 26119.

44. Americo Castro, *The Structure of Spanish History* (Princeton, N.J.: Princeton University Press, 1954), p. 582. Still, Vives never attained "plenary existence" in his attempt to harmonize the divine and the human, making of him a "squared circle" wherein his conflicting perspectives—the infinite and the finite, the one and the multiple—might be integrated. In a word, Vives was always en route, always in a state of growth and becoming.

45. Eugene Rice, *The Renaissance Idea of Wisdom* (Cambridge, Mass.: Harvard University Press, 1958); Antonio V. Romualdez, "Towards a History of the Renaissance Idea of Wisdom," *Studies in the Renaissance* 11 (1964): 133-50.

46. Rafael Altamira, *Cambridge Medieval History* (Cambridge, England: Cambridge University Press, 1932), vol. 5, *Spain, 1034-1248*, pp. 393-421; vol. 7, *Spain, 1252-1410*, pp. 567-98; vol. 8, *Spain, 1412-1516*, pp. 479-503. Also see Roger Bigelow Merriman, *The Rise of the Spanish Empire* (3 vols.; New York: Cooper Square Publishers, 1962), vol. 1, pp. 471-75; vol. 3, pp. 3-132, 182-88.

47. Roger Bigelow Merriman, "The Cortes of the Spanish Kingdoms in the Later Middle Ages," *American Historical Review* 16 (1911): 486-90.

48. Rafael Altamira, *A History of Spanish Civilization*, trans. P. Volkov (New York: Biblio & Tanner, 1968), p. 108.

49. S. M. Immamuddin, *Some Aspects of the Socio-Economic and Cultural History of Muslim Spain, 711-1492 A.D.* (Leiden: E. J. Brill, 1965), p. 56.

50. Ibid., pp. 58-59, 164. See also S. P. Scott, *History of the Moorish Empire in Europe* (3 vols.; Philadelphia, 1904), vol. 3, p. 516, in which reference is made to the public hospitals of Algeciras. Cordova had forty hospitals under Muhammed V. Suffering was regularly mitigated at the expense of the government and private philanthropy.

51. Richard Ford, *A Handbook for Travellers in Spain* (3 vols., reprint; Carbondale: Southern Illinois University Press, 1966), vol. 2, *Valencia*, pp. 642-88. This is a nineteenth-century prose painting of all of Spain, a highly personalized description.

52. Foster Watson, "The Influence of Valencia and Its Surroundings on the Later Life of Luis Vives as a Philosopher and as a Teacher," *Aberystwyth Studies* 9 (1927): 27-104. At the very moment in which Vives was writing *De Subventione*, Charles V was conclusively suppressing an uprising in Valencia of at least four years' duration. Earlier, Adrian (Charles's tutor in the Lowlands, a man destined for the papacy) had mishandled a situation, still further aggravated by Charles's refusal to enter the city. Through imperial action the Moors were forced into exile or to compulsory baptism; since many chose the former move, the internal development of the city—as well as the agricultural commerce built up by the Moors—slid into serious decline. See Merriman, *The Rise of the Spanish Empire*, 1:26-59, 106-32; Foster Watson, "Glamor of Renaissance Spain," in *Luis Vives: El Gran Valenciano* (Oxford: Oxford University Press, 1922), pp. 1-17.

53. Edward H. Flannery, *The Anguish of the Jews* (New York: Macmillan Co., 1965), pp. 131 ff.

54. Abdon M. Salazar, in *El Escudo de Armas de Juan Luis Vives* (London: Tamesis Books, 1967), notes that the family arms refer to their profession as merchants.

55. Castro, *The Structure of Spanish History*. Any insights of this essay into Vives's Spanish mind must necessarily be attributed to his analysis of the Hispanic genius resulting from nine centuries of Christian-Moorish-Jewish interaction.

56. Ibid., p. 520.

57. Ibid., p. 587. Thus Castro holds that he was incapable of isolating himself from his own distresses, consistently disinclined to seize fixed, serene ideas bound up in a closed system.

58. Ibid., p. 581.

59. Ibid., p. 571.

60. Ashley, *An Introduction*, 2:341.

61. Furnival, *Four Supplications*. See also the in-depth study by Frederic Morton Eden, *The State of the Poor* (3 vols.; London: J. Davis, 1797), in which an analysis of the conditions of the times is accompanied by local records.

62. Karl de Schweinitz, *England's Road to Social Security* (Philadelphia: University of Pennsylvania Press, 1943), p. 28. When he was bishop of London, Ridley had been the moving spirit of a committee that agitated and planned for relief. Other preachers included Thomas Lever, Henry Brinklow, and Hugh Latimer. Their task lay in convincing the larger population that desperate measures were necessary, contrary to the general attitude, which held that ample facilities for meeting economic trauma existed, that authorized begging would suffice, that assistance from the guilds was available, as well as almsgiving, titheing, parishes, and other private sources (ibid., p. 14).

63. Leonard, *Early History of English Poor-Relief*, p. 54.

64. George Nicholls, *A History of the English Poor Law* (3 vols.; Westminster: P. S. King & Sons, 1904), 1:924-1714. Each statute is clearly explained in this classic statement.

65. de Schweinitz, *England's Road to Social Security*, p. 14.

66.   The notion of localism and settlement played a role in all English legislation from the time of Richard I. Stringent residence requirements became more significant in the Tudor years and subsequently in the American colonies. See Richard Morris, *Government and Labor in Early America* (New York: Columbia University Press, 1946), p. 14, for original records.

67.   Ashley, *An Introduction*, p. 358.

68.   Ibid., p. 352. Ashley suggests that the fear of householders is contained in the old nursery rhyme:

> Hark! Hark! the dogs do bark,
> The beggars are coming to town,
> Some in rags and some in tags,
> And some in silken gowns.
> Some gave them white bread,
> Some gave them brown,
> And some gave them a good horse-whip,
> And sent them out of town.

However, the *Oxford Dictionary of Nursery Rhymes* (Oxford: Oxford University Press, 1952) traces the ditty to the "beggars," Dutchmen in the train of William III, 1688, with the velvet-gowned beggar referring to William himself. Katherine Elwes Thomas, in *The Real Personages of Mother Goose* (London, 1930), also touches on William, but prefers to think that the song first began when Prince Rupert's forces, a tattered Royal army, besieged the city of Bristol in 1653.

69.   Lens, *Poverty: America's Enduring Paradox*, p. 40.

70.   Among the best are Edith Abbott, *Public Assistance*, "Social Service Series" (Chicago: University of Chicago Press, 1940); Marcus Wilson Jernegan, *Laboring and Dependent Classes in Colonial America: 1607-1783* (Chicago: University of Chicago Press, 1931); Richard B. Morris, *Government and Labor in Early America* (New York: Octagon Books, 1965). Research has been carried out within the individual states; among the standard texts are Robert W. Kelso, *The History of Public Poor Relief in Massachusetts, 1620-1920* (New York: Houghton Mifflin Co., 1922); John L. Gillin, *History of Poor Relief Legislation in Iowa* (Iowa City, Iowa: State Historical Society, 1914), esp. chap. 1, "Poor Relief Legislation in the Northwest Territory and in Early Ohio," pp. 3-19; Roy M. Brown, *Public Poor Relief in North Carolina* (Chapel Hill: University of North Carolina Press, 1928); Grace A. Browning, *The Development of Poor Relief Legislation in Kansas*, "Social Service Monograph Series" (Chicago: University of Chicago Press, 1935); David A. Schneider, *The History of Public Welfare in New York State, 1609-1866*, "Social Service Monograph Series" (Chicago: University of Chicago Press, 1938).

71.   Jernegan, *Laboring and Dependent Classes*, p. 195. Jernegan is followed throughout this discussion since his work anticipates and confirms other authorities.

72.   Ibid., p. 195.

73.   Ibid., pp. 37-40.

74.   Ibid., p. 200.

75.   Ibid., pp. 175-88.

76.   Abbott, *Public Assistance*, p. 125.

77.   Ibid., p. 5.

78.   Ibid., pp. 5-6. At the time of her writing, Abbott held that pauper laws, as in Illinois, had not had extensive revisions since just after the Civil War. For an additional summary of the principles of poor relief in the colonies see Jernegan, *Laboring and Dependent Classes*, p. 208.

79.   See the annotations of Edith Abbott in *Public Assistance*, pp. 125-331.

80.   Typical of the pre-World War I optimism is Edward T. Devine, in *Misery and Its Causes* (New York: Macmillan Co., 1913). He takes the position that misery is not a punishment for immoral actions or the results of depraved character; rather, it is an economic condition that society may largely control.

81.   Abbott suggests that those conditions—a less democratic period of society, scattered home communities, the effectiveness of local government as the only authority which actually reached into the life of the ordinary citizen—are not contemporaneous and therefore do not permit the same social solutions (*Public Assistance*, p. 125).

82.   Salter, *Some Early Tracts*, pp. vii-xii. This is Sidney Webb's understanding of the historical phases of support for the poor.

Renaissance Society of America Reprint Texts